JENNIFER BOSWELL PICKENS

ISBN 978-0-615-58063-0

Library of Congress Control Number 2012939397


Printed in Canada.

100 Highland Park Village, Suite 200
Dallas, Texas 75205
fifeanddrumpress.com

*To my daughters*
*Abby, Maggie, Kate, and Ellie,*
*May you always love all of*
*God's creatures, great and small.*

# Table of Contents

# Foreword

by Barbara Bush

George and I loved our time at the White House surrounded by family, friends, and, of course, our pets. Millions of Americans followed the story of our beloved Millie, who had her first and only litter of puppies at the White House and then went on to write her own book. One of Millie's puppies, Spot, was born in the White House and later returned with George W. and Laura Bush.

Our dogs definitely didn't suffer from lack of attention at the White House. One man in particular made sure that our little ones were always happy. Dale Haney has cultivated relationships with all of the First Pets, going back to Richard Nixon's Irish setter, King Timahoe. Dale is now the superintendent of the White House Grounds, and he recently introduced me to Bo, the Obamas' Portuguese water dog.

In her wonderful book *Pets at the White House*, Jennifer Pickens has captured countless memories about the famous White House animals such as Liberty, Barney, Him and Her, Rex and Millie, and Buddy. Not only are these animals important to each First Family, but, as George points out, when you have the toughest job in the world, there is nothing like the unconditional love of a dog.

Barbara Bush

# Preface

My first book, *Christmas at the White House*, was inspired by memories of special Christmas holidays spent in my childhood home in Dallas. *Pets at the White House* is very much inspired by the animals we kept as pets during those years.

Growing up in my parents' old Southern-style house, I was always surrounded by animals. Of course we had the traditional ones, dogs. I had a black Lab named Sam and a cocker spaniel named Angel Star. I named her at the age of 3 after receiving her as a Christmas present. Occasionally I babysat my brother Jeff's golden retriever, Simba, who was named before the popular Disney movie came out. Later, when I was older, I had a golden retriever of my own, Bo, and a yellow Lab named Bea.

We also had several rabbits, including a black lop-eared named Herman my sister Julie gave me and a dwarf lop-eared named Thumper. I brought home Camper from Camp Longhorn, where I had earned the bunny with merits for being a good camper. Some of the rabbits reproduced, as they are known to do, and I lobbied my mom fiercely to keep the adorable bunnies, but we ended up giving them away.

I had a yellow canary, Tweety, a pocket parrot, and a regular-sized parrot we called Bos, after my dad. We added a guinea pig and a collection of hamsters to the mix, and, at any given moment, our aquarium was filled with all sorts of fish. The aquarium was in a fabulous oversized playroom with a large wall of windows that overlooked the back yard. Our home had both a pond and a creek, which were perfect for children—especially ones like me who loved wildlife. Tadpoles, collected from the pond, quickly turned into frogs.

We also kept a variety of turtles we found in the yard. I remember especially two small ones dubbed Red Stripe and Green Stripe. We were lucky enough to have all sorts of waterfowl, mainly wood ducks and mallards, which we fed every morning and watched from the kitchen windows while we ate. One morning, when my grandmother was visiting, we spied a great heron land and take a drink from the pond. My grandmother remarked that she felt like she was at the zoo.

I loved the days when my dad was home and he would teach me how to fish in our pond, which was full of bass, catfish, and more. There is no better activity a father and daughter can share. The stream that fed the creek was also home to the occasional crawfish and other creatures.

Once, when my brother was home from college, he found an injured pair of ducklings, so for several weeks we nursed them back to health before releasing them into the pond. The pond was also home to dramatically colored black swans. My favorite, Feathers, lived for nearly 20 years. She and her mate came from the Dallas Zoo.

Our yard was also home to a Canada goose and a funny-looking but sweet African goose named Barney that belonged to our neighbor. Barney waddled over to our pond so often that our neighbors finally gave him to us.

During the early days of summer, I would try to pet the baby ducks. By offering them bits of bread, eventually I earned the trust of a few. One year I thought it was a good idea to feed them from the dinner table, as we ate often on the back porch. When several of the ducks – as well as the swans – attempted to make their way into the house, we decided that wasn't the best idea.

Our most exotic pet was a barn owl, which my brother rescued during a hunting trip. I loved him! He was beautiful, with a white heart-shaped face and light brown and gray feathers on his back. We hoped to release him into the wild eventually, but he became dependent upon us. So we built an atrium for him in the back yard, and, at times, he was kept on a tether. We had to hold him wearing special gloves, to protect us from his talons. Because barn owls are smaller, it was fun to let him sit on our arms. One summer we even drove him to South Padre with us on a family vacation, as he was truly part of the Boswell clan.

Our family was so well-known for our pets that one Christmas the doorbell rang, and there was a small black billy goat on the front porch with a red bow and bell tied around its neck. My brother's friends thought it would be funny to give my mom a goat, because they figured they had found the one animal she wouldn't keep. She, however, took him in happily. We named him Black Belt, and it wasn't until he thought it was fun to jump on cars that we decided it was best for him to live elsewhere.

My best friend from elementary school and I tested my mom again when we brought home two chickens from our fourth-grade graduation. At school we learned about business by raising chickens and selling their eggs. When we graduated, we were allowed to keep our chickens, which of course we wanted to do. My mom, as usual, accepted them with a smile. It was fun for a while, but eventually the chickens became a problem for the other animals, so, like the goat, my mother found an alternate home for them.

Now that I am grown and have a family of my own, we have a family dog named Annabelle. Like most golden retrievers, she has been a wonderful and loving companion to my husband, Bryan, and me and our four girls. We helped Annabelle fight cancer bravely several years ago, and she has been one of the few dogs to beat t-cell lymphoma. During our many trips to the vet for her treatments, we met many other dedicated, loving pet owners. It's for them, and for all of you, that I wanted to write this book.

You can tell so much about people by the pets they keep and cherish as members of their families. *Pets at the White House* gives us a glimpse into the personal side of the American presidency in ways no other history book can. It's through these stories and photographs that we get to know each President and his family with some of their favorite friends—their pets.

# *Introduction*

I hope you enjoy this compilation of 50 years of pets that have lived in the President's house. The animals pictured on these pages, and their accompanying stories, reveal as much about these 10 heads of state, First Ladies, and sometimes their children as they do about the historic times in which they lived. They even reflect the First Families' individual tastes, personalities, and social and political priorities.

The book begins with the Kennedy family. Macaroni, First Daughter Caroline's pony, remains one of the most iconic White House pets of all time, and it's just one of the animals from this First Family's large menagerie. For years pets have been celebrated and adored at 1600 Pennsylvania Avenue, and during the half-century chronicled in this retrospective, they reached new heights of popularity—with the help of the ever-changing media and its outlets, as well as Americans' growing affection for animal companions.

Of course, famous presidential pets of all kinds date back to the earliest years of our Republic, when the varied assortments of animals living at the Executive Mansion mirrored those found in many Americans' homes. Therefore horses, cows, goats, chickens, and even sheep could be found at the White House, along with the more domestic animals such as dogs, cats, birds, and other small pets.

George Washington loved his animals. Naturally he had horses and many dogs, as well as livestock, on his much-loved Mount Vernon in Virginia, but Washington never actually lived at the White House. He did receive a gift from the King of Spain: a pair of donkeys. Only one survived the voyage, and the President named him Royal Gift. Washington spent much time and effort breeding the donkey with his American mares, creating top-of-the-line mules. Washington's wife favored smaller animals and indulged a green parrot. When third President Thomas Jefferson sent Meriwether Lewis and William Clark on their famous 1803 expedition to explore the West, they dispatched a variety of animals—both live and dead—for the President to study. The most memorable were two grizzly bear cubs that he kept in a cage at the White House. Jefferson's pet mockingbird, Dick, was often allowed to fly freely around the President's office (now the State Dining Room) and would sit on his master's shoulder. Jefferson was also an architect, and he installed the famous horse stables that are now part of the West Colonnade. One story that cannot be confirmed is that during Marquis de Lafayette's month-long stay as a guest of President and Mrs. John Quincy Adams in 1825 at the Executive Mansion, the visiting dignitary was given the gift of an alligator, which he kept in the bathroom of the East Room.

Like other presidents of the 19th century, Andrew Jackson was a famous horseman, and in fact our seventh President was the only one to operate a racing stable at the White House. The 12th President, Zachary Taylor, had a horse, Old Whitney was often spotted grazing on the White House lawn. Visitors would sometimes pluck hairs from his tail as souvenirs. President Abraham Lincoln's sons Tad and Willie preferred riding their beloved ponies over all other activities. Sadly, following the death of Willie, Tad was too heartsick to ride, so the President acquired pet goats

**Left**
Sheep graze on the White House lawn, circa 1919. It was common through the early 1900s to have livestock at the White House.

**Below**
President Taft's famous cow, Pauline Wayne (Queen of the Capital Cows), grazing the White House lawn, in front of the State, War and Navy Building (now known as the Eisenhower Executive Office Building), circa 1909.

**Above**
Archie Roosevelt, son of President Theodore Roosevelt, on his calico Shetland pony Algonquin, in front of the new White House offices, circa 1903.

Nanko and Nanny, who roamed freely at the White House. Despite Mrs. Lincoln's objections to the animals, both the President and Tad found much joy in them. Tad, of course, is also often credited with saving his pet turkey, Jack, from being turned into Christmas dinner by bursting into a cabinet meeting in tears and pleading with his father to spare the bird. It's a story often cited by presidents at the annual pardoning of the turkey at Thanksgiving.

President and Mrs. Rutherford B. Hayes and their family maintained a menagerie that consisted of a goat, four canaries, two German shepherds, an English mastiff, four kittens, two hunting dogs, and a mockingbird. Hayes also took pride in his pedigreed Jersey cows. En masse, they were often referred to as "Lucy's ark," after the First Lady. The family's love for animals became so apparent that David B. Sickels, a U.S. diplomat at the consulate in Bangkok, sent the Hayeses' daughter, Fanny, a Siamese cat. Siam, as she was named, was the first of the breed to be sent to the United States.

President Benjamin Harrison's administration included a houseful of pets as well. The most notable was Old Whiskers, a goat so rambunctious that one day the President was forced to chase him down Pennsylvania Avenue when the animal decided to run away— pulling the First Grandchildren along with him in a cart.

One of the most celebrated animal lovers of the 20th century was Theodore Roosevelt, the 26th President. Roosevelt, along with his six children, moved into America's House with an ever-evolving menagerie of pets. Over time, the mix included a pony, sheep, dogs, cats, a macaw, guinea pigs, two kangaroo rats, a snake, a black bear, and a one-legged rooster—and that's just a partial list. In 1908 the *Washington Evening Star* observed: "There is no home in Washington so full of pets of high and low degree as is the White House, and those pets not only occupy the attention of the children, but the President is himself their good friend, and has a personal interest in every one of them."

The Roosevelts also loved horses, and one of the most famous was certainly Algonquin, an Icelandic calico Shetland pony that belonged to their son Archie. When Archie became very ill with the measles, his brothers Quentin and Kermit—with the help of footman Charlie Reeder—thought the best way to cheer him up would be a visit from his pony. Thus, the story of a pony being snuck up to the private residence of the second floor of the White House by way of elevator became legend.

Another famous Roosevelt pet tale involved a six-toed cat named Slippers. After a formal dinner, President Roosevelt was escorting the wife of an ambassador from the State Dining Room when he came upon Slippers—stretched out in the middle of the hallway purring. Rather than simply moving the feline, the President opted to lead the woman around the cat, forcing the line of ambassadors and ministers behind him to follow suit. The President preferred what he called "Heinz pickle" dogs from multiple bloodlines. One of his favorites was Skip, a short-legged, black-and-tan mongrel terrier brought home from a Colorado bear hunt.

Until the beginning of the 19th century it was common to find cows at the White House, as D.C. had no dairy or delivery companies. President William Taft, the 27th President, was the last to keep a cow on the lawn of the White House grounds to provide milk and butter. Her name was Pauline Wayne, a.k.a. "Queen of the Capital Cows," and she was quite famous during her day. Pauline was a handsome Holstein, whose pasture was the grassy area by the State, War and Navy Building (now known as the Eisenhower Executive Office Building). Setting an example to all Americans during World War I, President Woodrow Wilson had sheep graze the White House lawn so the gardeners could serve their country. One sheep was famously named Old Ike. Unfortunately, it was not just the lawn these sheep enjoyed; they also feasted on the shrubbery and flowerbeds. Yet they were praised for their patriotism when their wool was auctioned off, benefiting the American Red Cross and Salvation Army.

One of the first celebrity pets to live in the White House was Laddie Boy, faithful friend of our 29th President, Warren G. Harding. Laddie Boy—or Caswell Laddie Boy, his full pedigree name—was an Airedale terrier. He moved into the Executive Mansion in 1921 and made himself right at home. He even had his own

**Left**
Major Russell Harrison, son of President Benjamin Harrison, with his daughter, niece, nephew, dog, and goat Old Whiskers on the White House South Lawn, circa 1890.

**Below**
President Theodore Roosevelt, a great animal lover, and his six children lived in the White House from 1901-1909. Among the family's many pets was Rollo, a Saint Bernard, circa 1906.

**Above**
President Harding with First Dog Laddie Boy, being photographed in front of the White House, June 13, 1922. Laddie Boy, an Airedale, was the most famous of President Harding's pets.

**Bottom Left**
First Lady Grace Coolidge, holding her pet raccoon, Rebecca. The President and First Lady loved Rebecca and often walked her on a leash.

**Bottom Right**
President and Mrs. Coolidge with their two dogs, Rob Roy and Prudence Prim receiving children at the Easter Egg Roll, April 1925.

**Opposite**
Thousands of copies of this portrait of President Herbert Hoover and his dog King Tut were distributed throughout the country in a successful attempt to make him appear more charismatic to secure the presidential election of 1928.

**Right**
First Dog Fala, President Franklin D. Roosevelt's terrier, one of the best loved and most famous presidential pets of all time, photographing the photographers at the White House, April 7, 1942.

**Above**
President Dwight D. Eisenhower and his Weimaraner, Heidi, walk back to the White House, March 11, 1959.

**Opposite Top**
Feller, a blond cocker spaniel, was an unsolicited 1947 Christmas gift to President Truman. The Trumans elected to give away the puppy.

**Opposite Bottom**
President Franklin D. Roosevelt driving in his convertible with his dog, Fala, through Hyde Park, October 24, 1944.

hand-carved chair to sit in during cabinet meetings and often waited on the front steps of the White House to greet official delegations. He served as formal host of the White House Easter Egg Roll in 1923, filling in during President and Mrs. Harding's absence. The White House hosted birthday parties for the dog, complete with dog-biscuit cake. Laddie Boy often made the press, and sometimes the papers would quote him in "interviews," especially when the events of the day were comparatively dull. Following the President's untimely death in 1923, newspaper carriers collected 19,134 pennies to be melted and sculpted into a statue of Laddie Boy. Harding's widow died before the statue was completed in 1927, so the finished work was presented to the Smithsonian Institution, where it currently resides.

After President Harding's death, *The New York Times* reported: "When the presidential automobile drew up under the porte-cochere before the north door, Laddie Boy bounded out and down the steps in greeting so cordial and affectionate that both President Calvin Coolidge and his wife, Grace, took special notice of it. Coolidge, relating the incident, said that he hoped it might be regarded as 'an omen of the spirit in which he was received by all those associated with the late President.'"

President and Mrs. Coolidge had perhaps the largest menagerie of pets the White House has ever seen. It would be nearly impossible to list every pet from the vast and diverse collection, as many were received as presents from friends, donations from the general public, or gifts from heads of state. The Coolidges' love for animals became so widely known that the American public actually began to send them their unwanted pets. Throughout Coolidge's term in office, the First Couple received dogs, cats, a flock of birds, a raccoon, a baby bear, a wallaby, a pair of lions, an antelope, a goose, a donkey, a pigmy hippo, and even a bobcat. One of the most memorable had to be Rebecca, the raccoon, a favorite pet of the First Couple. She walked on a leash and had a special house built just for her. The Coolidge dogs alone numbered more than a dozen. Rob Roy was the Presidents favorite and will forever be immortalized in Mrs. Coolidge's portrait that hangs at the White House. Another white collie, Prudence Prim, was the First Lady's most revered, and she was known for dressing the dog in hats. As the President once said, "Any man who does not like dogs and want them about does not deserve to be in the White House."

Our 31st President, Herbert Hoover, was an equally avid dog lover. Following campaign advice, with hopes of shaping his image into something warmer and more charismatic, he released a photograph of himself with his German shepherd, King Tut. Thousands of signed copies circulated around the country of the smiling presidential hopeful holding up the paws of his dog—and it worked. Hoover won the presidency with a decisive victory, and King Tut, along with his master, moved into the First Residence. With them came a pack of other dogs, which included Big Ben and Sonnie, two fox terriers; Glen the Scotch collie; Yukon; Eskimo dog Eaflehurst Gillette; Pat, a setter; another shepherd/police dog; Weeje the elkhound; and finally Patrick, the huge Irish wolfhound, whose formal name was Cragwood Padraic.

Franklin D. Roosevelt, our iconic 32nd President, was master to the equally notorious Scottish terrier Fala, who captured the attention of the American public and became key to Roosevelt's public image. Fala appeared in photos and traveled with the President, attended galas with world leaders, and even received fan mail from children across the country. Once, when Fala accompanied the President on a Naval destroyer, the sailors had wanted souvenirs, so they clipped bits of hair off the pooch. An MGM film about a typical day in the White House featured Fala, and she became an honorary private in the U.S. Army by "contributing" $1 to the war effort for every day of the year, setting an example for others on the homefront. During the Battle of the Bulge, American soldiers used the word Fala as a sort of codeword, a supplementary safeguard against German soldiers attempting to infiltrate American ranks. Fala even found herself in the middle of the 1944 presidential campaign, when Roosevelt addressed some rampant rumors in the now-famous Fala Speech he delivered to the International Brotherbood of Teamsters, Chauffeurs, Warehousemen and Helpers of America. Rumor had it that Roosevelt had accidentally left Fala behind on the Aleutian Islands while on tour there and had sent a U.S. Navy destroyer to retrieve him at an exorbitant (taxpayer-funded) cost. He countered the hearsay: "These Republican leaders have not been content with attacks on me, or my wife, or on my sons. No, not content with that, they now include my little dog, Fala. Well, of course, I don't resent attacks, and my family doesn't resent attacks—but Fala does resent them. You know, Fala is Scotch, and being a Scottie, as soon as he learned that the Republican fiction writers in Congress and out had concocted a story that I'd left him behind on an Aleutian Island and had sent a destroyer back to find him—at a cost to the taxpayers of two or three, or eight or 20 million dollars—his Scotch soul was furious. He has not been the same dog since. I am accustomed to hearing malicious falsehoods about myself—such as that old, worm-eaten chestnut that I have represented myself as indispensable. But I think I have a right to resent, to object, to libelous statements about my dog!" The crowd went wild, and he went on to win the election. Fala became so well-known that he became a bit of a security risk, because anytime he was spotted on a train platform, the public knew the President was nearby. He contributed to the war effort, giving up his rubber toys and bones to help promote a nationwide scrap rubber collection campaign. Fala survived Roosevelt by seven years and was buried next to him. A statue of the dog alongside Roosevelt is prominently featured in Washington, D.C.'s Franklin Delano Roosevelt Memorial.

"If you want a friend in Washington, get a dog," said the 33rd President, Harry Truman–and most did. This book highlights the past five decades through portraits of our presidents and their families—with their pets—in quiet moments of reflection and boisterous moments of fun. Animals have played a role in forming perceptions of the character and personalities of our presidents. They're captured here through 50 years of magnificent photographs taken by White House photographers and others. As you read, be reminded of our nation's great heritage and take special pride in the White House, America's House, and some of its most fascinating tenants—the First Pets.

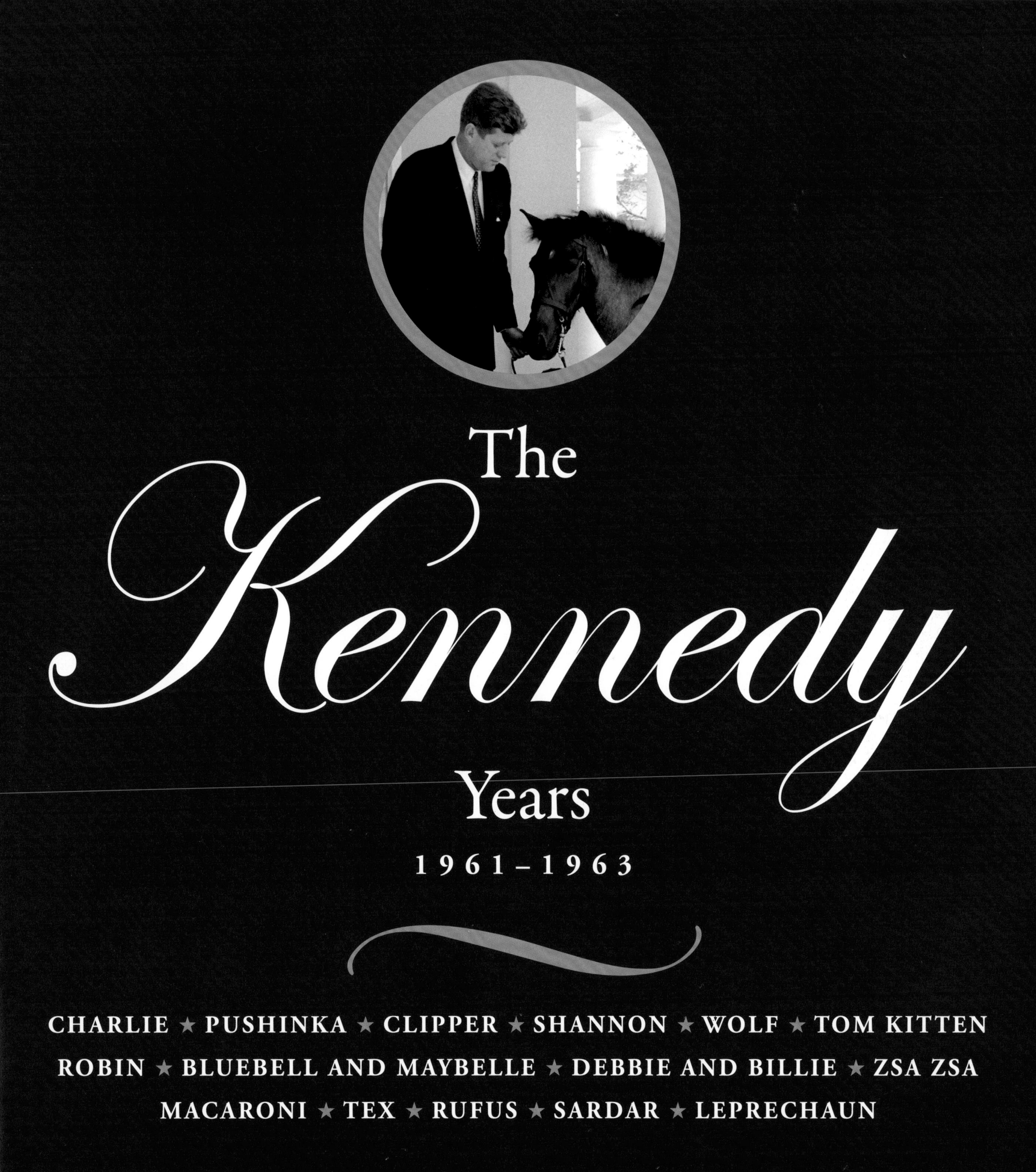
The
Kennedy
Years
1961–1963
CHARLIE ★ PUSHINKA ★ CLIPPER ★ SHANNON ★ WOLF ★ TOM KITTEN
ROBIN ★ BLUEBELL AND MAYBELLE ★ DEBBIE AND BILLIE ★ ZSA ZSA
MACARONI ★ TEX ★ RUFUS ★ SARDAR ★ LEPRECHAUN

**President John F. Kennedy** was the youngest candidate ever to be elected to the Office of President of the United States, in 1960. He, along with First Lady Jacqueline Bouvier Kennedy, wanted to make the White House an appropriate museum for a head of state while maintaining an atmosphere fitting for their two small children, Caroline and John Jr. To that end, the young First Family filled their home with a menagerie of animals, ranging from dogs, cats, birds, and hamsters to ponies, parakeets, ducks, and more. In fact, the Kennedys had the largest pack of dogs at the White House since the days of President Theodore Roosevelt. From Inauguration Day on, Americans were enthralled with this energetic First Family—and their pets.

President and Mrs. Kennedy both had a deep love of animals dating back to their youngest days. Mrs. Kennedy grew up with horses, rabbits, and dogs and even raised her own 4-H calf—and she wanted similarly enriching experiences for her children. When the Kennedy family entered the Executive Mansion, along with them came Charlie, a Welsh terrier who had been with the family for two years. They also had a cat named Tom Kitten, a canary named Robin, a couple of parakeets named Bluebelle and Maybelle, and a few hamsters. Two ponies, Macaroni and Leprechaun (the latter was John Jr.'s Connemara pony and a gift from the people of Ireland) would soon be joined by a third called Tex, a gift from Vice President Lyndon B. Johnson. A revolving door of pets was a constant throughout the Kennedys' days at 1600 Pennsylvania Avenue.

Despite his severe allergy to animal hair, the President, too, wanted the children to have all the animals they desired, and he enjoyed them as well. At dusk, if he was still working, he would walk outside onto the South Lawn and clap his hands. The children would shriek with joy and the dogs would bark as they all came running toward him, and he would pass around candy and dog treats. He is often cited as being the first President to have a dog greet him upon his arrival when Marine One would land at the White House. According to Traphes Bryant, a longtime Executive Residence staffer and electrician—as well as the First Family's dog handler—"JFK got a kick out of being welcomed back to the White House by a dog. Others were thrilled to be greeted by the President; the President in turn wanted to be greeted by a dog. He was never too tired to pet the dog I would have there as he came off the ramp."

The Kennedys were given many pets as presents. One of the more famous ones they received was Pushinka. The name means "fluffy" in Russian, and the dog was a gift from Soviet Premier Nikita Khrushchev when he visited the United States and the White House following the Cuban Missile Crisis. The pup's mother, Strelka, had been the first Russian dog in space, and Pushok, a dog who had been used in many Soviet ground experiments, was the sire.

Pushinka endeared herself not just to young Caroline and John Jr. but also to Charlie, Caroline's

## THE SPY WHO LICKED THEM

Pushinka, one of the most famous presidential gifts of all time, was a white dog given to the Kennedy family by Soviet Premier Nikita Khrushchev. Some were suspicious of the dog at first, fearing she might be a Russian spy. But after going through a battery of tests at Walter Reed Army Medical Center that ruled out any hidden listening devices, microphones, germs, or bombs, she became a cherished family pet.

**Preceding Pages**
Caroline Kennedy sits proudly on her pony Macaroni, on the South Lawn, March 30, 1962.

Kennedy dogs Charlie and Pushinka on the South Lawn, June 22, 1961.

**Right**
Pushinka and her brood, which President Kennedy affectionately referred to as "pupniks," July 9, 1963.

**Opposite**
The entire JFK clan–canines included–on vacation in Cape Cod. Pictured are Clipper the German shepherd, Charlie the Welsh terrier, Wolf the Irish wolfhound, Shannon the Irish spaniel, and Pushinka's puppies. Caroline leans on Shannon while playing with Charlie, John Jr. pets the pups, and Jackie holds Clipper.

terrier. The two dogs eventually mated, and the President referred to the offspring as "pupniks." Mrs. Kennedy and the children were in Hyannis Port for the summer when the litter was born, so the President arranged for the pups to go there for a visit. The President himself choreographed an elaborate surprise entrance, and the children were soon happily playing beside the ocean with the dogs. There were four "pupniks" in all: Butterfly, White Tips, Blackie, and Streaker. One was given to the Lawfords, the President's sister Patricia and her husband, actor Peter Lawford. Another remained at the Kennedy home on Squaw Island. Butterfly and Streaker were given to the winners of a children's essay contest orchestrated by the First Lady. In order to win one of the dogs, the child had to describe how to care for a dog properly and detail the type of home or environment the animal should reside in. More than 10,000 letters were received. The most famous was unsigned, and the child simply stated, "I will raise the dog to be a Democrat and bite all Republicans."

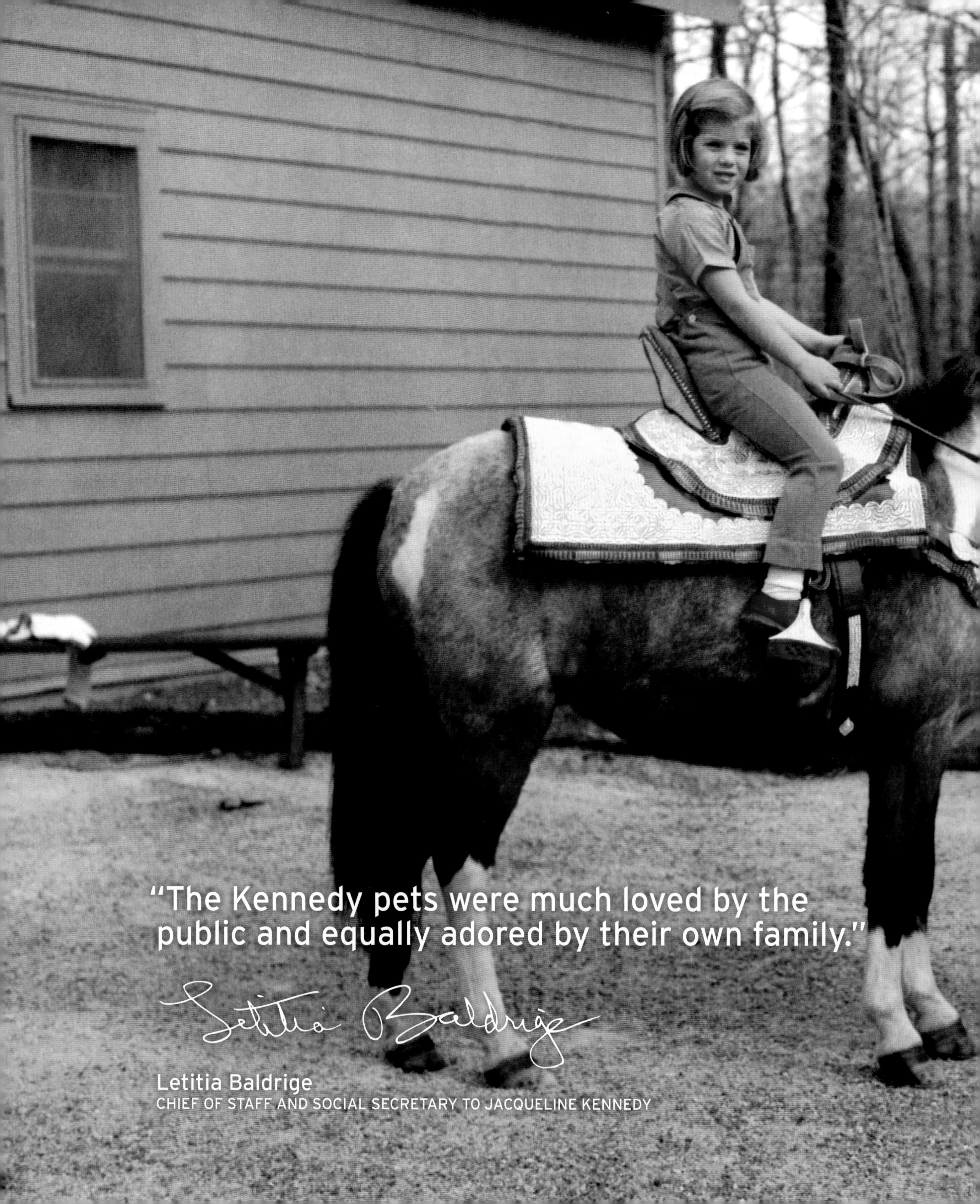

"The Kennedy pets were much loved by the public and equally adored by their own family."

Letitia Baldrige

CHIEF OF STAFF AND SOCIAL SECRETARY TO JACQUELINE KENNEDY

**Preceding Pages**
President Kennedy with his family at Camp David, Maryland. Caroline rides Macaroni while John Jr. holds his mother's hand as he reaches out to the horse, March 31, 1963.

**Right**
On the South Lawn during a children's picnic, John Jr. climbs down a ladder at the White House, as nurse Maude Shaw, an unidentified White House worker, and Charlie look on, June 7, 1963.

**Below**
The young President relaxes with his dog Mo in Hyannis Port after winning the nomination for Congress in the 11th Massachusetts District, June 23, 1946.

The Kennedy family also received their share of more exotic animal gifts. After Caroline and her friends saw the Disney movie *Bambi*, her parents began to look into acquiring a pet deer for the 3-year-old. The President of Ireland, Éamon de Valera, beat them to the punch, sending a pair to the family. But after learning about caring for deer in captivity and warnings of the animals' temperamental tendencies, the family decided that the deer should live at the zoo.

The deer were not the only animals that left the Executive Mansion under unfortunate circumstances. Caroline, sadly, had to give up Tom Kitten. The cat was particularly fond of the President, but his allergies eventually meant the kitten had to go. So Tom was given to Mrs. Kennedy's secretary, Mary Gallagher, who also had small children. The hamsters, however, fared far worse. At one point, several of them ended up in the President's bathtub, where one drowned.

**Left**
Caroline Kennedy's pet ducks waddle across the White House lawn, June 22, 1961.

**Below**
Inside the White House, Caroline holds Tom Kitten, October 31, 1963.

And when hamsters Debbie and Billy became parents, Billy turned on the six babies, as hamsters can do. Debbie apparently became so enraged that she retaliated against Billy, and in the tussle, they both unfortunately perished. The hamsters were not the only pets whose fate took a somber note. Caroline's canary, Robin, also died while the family was in the White House. A ceremony, complete with pomp and circumstance, was conducted on the South Lawn, and Caroline on occasion showed visitors the grave. And then there was Zsa Zsa. The white rabbit, sent to the Kennedys by a magician from Pennsylvania, allegedly drank beer and played the first five bars of "The Star Spangled Banner" on a golden toy trumpet. Despite her presumed talent, she and her trumpet were promptly sent to live at an orphanage.

Other dogs would join the Kennedys as well. A German shepherd named Clipper was a gift to Jackie Kennedy from her father-in-law, Ambassador Joseph P. Kennedy. President de Valera sent an Irish cocker spaniel, Shannon, to

**Right**
President Kennedy greets a deer, September 1963.

**Opposite**
President Kennedy visits with his son, daughter, and pony Macaroni outside the Oval Office in the West Wing Colonnade, June 22, 1962.

**Left**
First Lady Jacqueline Kennedy stands outside the White House in the Rose Garden with her dog Clipper, her sister Lee Radziwill, and Lee's daughter Christina, January 15, 1963.

the First Family (probably thinking it a more suitable pet than a deer). An Irish priest bearing the same name—Kennedy—gave the family an enormous wolfhound (the largest and tallest of the galloping hound breeds) named Wolf. He was great with people but had trouble getting along with other dogs. Each of the canines had its own distinct personality. Charlie was the President's favorite, and the dog seemed to know it. He swam with the President in the White House pool and growled whenever another dog went through a doorway before him—much to the amusement of the Commander in Chief.

The Kennedys were perhaps best known for their horses and ponies. Mrs. Kennedy, an accomplished rider, was probably the most proficient horsewoman in White House history, and she wanted to teach her children to feed, groom, and saddle their own mounts. So three ponies—Macaroni, Leprechaun, and Tex—went back and forth between the White House and Glen Ora, the Kennedy estate in Virginia. People loved to stop and watch through the iron fence of the White House as the ponies roamed freely on the South Lawn eating grass. Tex was a 3-year-old gelding, a Yucatan bay pony, brown with one black shoe. Macaroni, a 10-year-old gelding, part

**Right**
The Kennedy and Radziwill families in Palm Beach, Florida, on Christmas Day 1962.

**Left**
Caroline rides on the White House lawn with a White House escort—dad JFK—by her side, June 22, 1962.

**Right**
John Jr. plays with one of the "pupnik" puppies at Squaw Island in Hyannis Port, August 3, 1963.

**Opposite**
The First Lady and John Jr. ride her favorite horse, Sardar (a gift from Pakistan President Mohammad Ayub Khan), while Caroline rides Tex (a gift from Vice President Lyndon B. Johnson), at Glen Ora in Middleburg, Virginia, November 19, 1962.

Shetland, roan with four white stockings and star, was the first horse that Caroline learned to ride. Macaroni was the most loved by the public and often posed for pictures with the President and the children (usually while Mrs. Kennedy was away, as she frowned on having the children's and pets' photos taken for political gain). Macaroni became so popular that he began to receive an enormous amount of fan mail, which made a real mark in White House pet history.

One afternoon, while working in the Oval Office, President Kennedy looked up to find Macaroni peering at him through the window. The two stared at each other thoughtfully for some time, and then, as the story goes, the President smiled and opened the door to invite the pony inside. The pony considered it for a few moments and then simply turned around and walked away. He would have been the first horse to enter the West Wing.

Mrs. Kennedy had a horse of her own as well. After she paid a state visit to Pakistan, President Mohammed Ayub Khan sent the First Lady a gorgeous bay gelding named Sardar, which became her favorite horse. Sardar was always kept at Glen Ora. President Khan also offered an elephant and a few tiger cubs, which the First Lady politely declined.

Margaret Truman, President Truman's daughter, perhaps most accurately described the Kennedys' days at the White House with their pets: "All in all, the Kennedy family made good use of the White House. It's a marvelous place for children—young children—to run and shriek and ride a pony, play with dogs, cats, and hamsters. They ranged over the whole house and enormous grounds. Even in the playschool, in the solarium on the third floor, or on the roof over the Truman Balcony, the children could raise rabbits and ride their bicycles. Children don't have to worry about the bigger problems faced by the President, but he could take enormous delight in watching their pleasure in playing with their pets."

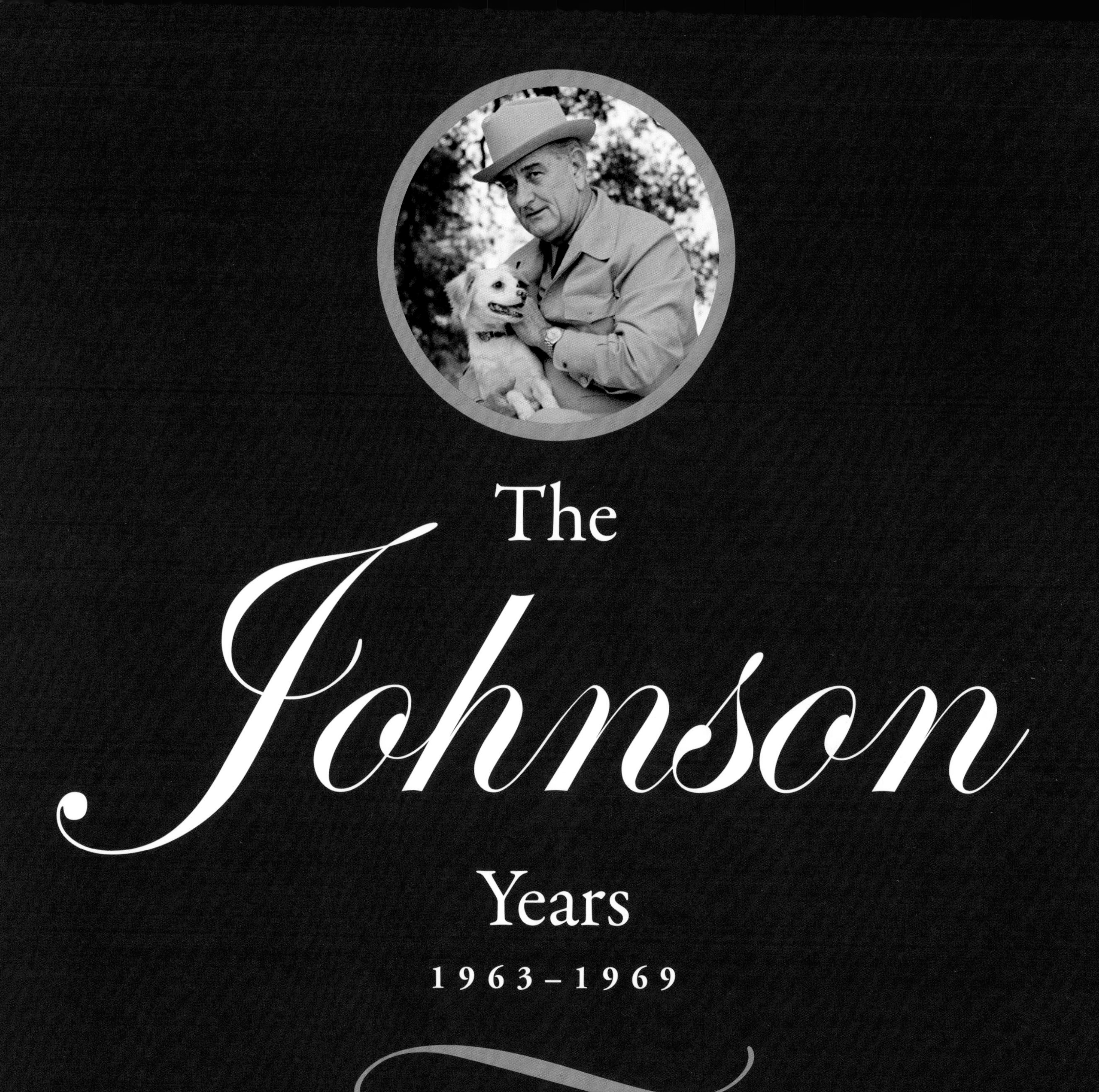

# The Johnson Years

## 1963–1969

**HIM AND HER ★ EDGAR ★ BLANCO ★ FRECKLES ★ YUKI**

**President Lyndon Johnson** and Lady Bird Johnson brought to the White House an immeasurable amount of authentic Texas-style energy—often exhibited in the President's genuine and unabashed love of his pets, ranging from purebred beagles to a mutt picked up at a roadside gas station.

Like many boys growing up in the Texas Hill Country, Lyndon B. Johnson had pets as a child. He received his first dog, Rover, at the age of 4. The President-to-be was a beagle admirer long before the breed became fashionable, and while he was senator (and later Vice President) his daughter's beagle became popular with the public. It was named Little Beagle Johnson—in keeping with the LBJ-initial theme prevalent throughout the family, including Johnson's wife, Lady Bird Johnson, and his two daughters, Lynda Bird and Luci Baines.

Little Beagle Johnson, nicknamed Old Beagle Johnson in his later years, lived to be 15 and was a devoted companion to the Johnson family. Johnson was so crushed when the beagle died that he had him cremated and could not part with the remains. He left the ashes in a box above the refrigerator, and it was not until the family cook, Zephyr Wright, found out what was in the box that they were removed and buried in a special plot on the Johnsons' Texas ranch.

Circumstances were far from jubilant when the Johnsons entered the White House on December 7, 1963. The move was orchestrated quietly and with minimal fanfare, as it coincided with a month of mourning proclaimed by President Johnson following President Kennedy's assassination. Luci drove beagles Him and Her to their new residence at 1600 Pennsylvania Avenue.

Other dogs came to the White House during the Johnson Administration (along with an assortment of hamsters and birds), but it was Him and Her, Luci's beagle duo, that the President doted on early in his presidency and that *Life* magazine proclaimed "the most talked about canines since FDR's Fala took office." The beagles were even more talked about in April 1964. At a meeting with some financial experts, the President took the press on a walk around the White House grounds to meet Him and Her. He picked up one of the dogs by the ears, prompting a couple of quick yelps—and a public outcry from a nation of dog lovers. It made the front pages of most of the country's newspapers and dominated the covers of magazines. The White House was flooded with telegrams, mail, and phone calls. The press obsessed over the story, and reporters polled veterinarians and other animal experts from the American Kennel Club, National Beagle Club, and American Society for the Prevention of Cruelty to Animals. Some defended the President, while others condemned the act. However, the dogs had their own opinion on the matter. Him and Her were doing just fine, and it was well-known around the White House just how much the President

**Preceding Page**
President Johnson, led by Yuki (who was found at a Texas gas station), boards Marine One on the White House lawn, with Lady Bird following, September 28, 1967.

**Opposite**
President Johnson demonstrates for the press his controversial—yet harmless—beagle ear-lift stunt.

**Left**
Him and Her sit on the South Lawn of the White House. Both wear "LBJ for the USA" campaign buttons, October 14, 1964.

**Below**
Charles Robb, Lynda Johnson, Lady Bird Johnson, Luci Johnson Nugent (holding the dog Yuki), and Patrick Nugent.

loved the pair. As *Life* reported, "Whether or not they approve of the President's way of demonstrating his affection, they [the dogs] probably wouldn't swap places with any other dogs in the world. Not many dogs have been privileged to shoo birds off the White House lawn, get underfoot at a cabinet meeting, or mingle with dignitaries at a state ball."

The beagle pair swam with the President in the White House pool, joining the family on trips to Camp David, and sometimes were included in meetings with visiting heads of state. Photos were given out, most often to children, of the President with the two pups. President Johnson, as a true Texan, also showed his affection toward the dogs by providing them with luxury housing, seeking bigger and better doghouses for them throughout his term.

Early on, the beagles acquired a canine accomplice. Just a few days after the President and First Lady's arrival at the White House, a 9-year-old girl named Lois Nelson of Woodstock, Illinois, sent the couple a 6-month-old pure-white collie. The President called the pup Blanco, the name of a small town near his Texas ranch and also the Spanish word for "white." (The dog's registered name was Leader Blair Jamie of Edlen.) The President graciously accepted the dog, but he made it clear that Blanco would be symbolic of all the wonderful dogs that had been offered to the First Family from around the country, which would have to be returned, as he could not accept every such generous gesture. Blanco was born July 19, 1963, and his pure white color made him rare. Blanco was a nervous dog and a bit of a biter. He once bit his beagle companion Him, causing quite a scare, and later sunk his teeth into Edgar (another beagle who joined the First Family in the White House), injuring his nose so

**Opposite**
The President and his grandson, Lyndon Nugent, play with Yuki at the LBJ Ranch near Johnson City, Texas, June 1, 1968.

**Above Left**
Reporters trail the President and First Lady as they stroll through D.C. with Him and Her, August 24, 1964.

**Above Right**
During a Keep America Beautiful presentation, Lady Bird shakes hands with Lassie before White House onlookers, May 3, 1967.

"LBJ's favorite dog was a rescue named Yuki, a white mutt who had been abandoned by his owner at a gas station in LBJ's hometown of Johnson City, Texas. They shared a very significant bond that personified the American spirit: only in America could a poor boy from Johnson City end up in the White House."

Lyndon Nugent
GRANDSON OF PRESIDENT AND MRS. JOHNSON

## DOG FIGHT

One of the more memorable stories involving Yuki took place once Richard Nixon had secured the nomination as the Republican candidate for President. Nixon flew to President Johnson's ranch for a briefing on the war. As Nixon was departing, Yuki boarded the helicopter and crawled under Nixon's seat. President Johnson went aboard the chopper to get Yuki and reportedly said to Nixon, "Look, you've got my helicopter, you're after my job, and now you want my dog!" On the day of Nixon's inauguration, during the historic transfer of power, the two presidents laughed about the incident, and Nixon told Johnson, "I told you I wanted your job, not your dog."

**Preceding Pages**
The President introduces the puppies (sired by Him) to Courtney Valenti, daughter of Jack Valenti, while Blanco watches in the background.

**Left**
LBJ croons with Yuki as Ambassador David Bruce looks on, February 6, 1968.

**Opposite Top**
Kim, another of the LBJ beagles, looks over the shoulder of Colonel James U. Cross, President Johnson's pilot, aboard Air Force One, November 19, 1966.

**Opposite Bottom**
Lady Bird, the President, Luci Nugent, and Lyndon Nugent with Freckles, Kim, Him, and Blanco in the White House Rose Garden, April 22, 1966.

**Left**
President Johnson spends his birthday in the pool at the LBJ Ranch with grandson Lyndon Nugent and Yuki, August 27, 1968.

badly that it required stitches. Despite these outbursts, Johnson's love for Blanco never wavered.

Sadly, the female beagle Her passed away when she was little more than a year old. After accidentally swallowing a small rock, she died on the operating table. The President was devastated. For some time only two dogs resided at the Executive Mansion, Him and Blanco, who were Nos. 1 and 2 of Washington's Top 10 Dogs. Their license tags ranked them accordingly, as a low license number was a great status symbol in Washington, D.C.

Him sired a litter of five puppies born in October 1965. President Johnson's daughter Luci kept two of the pups, Kim and Freckles, whose original name was Pecosa, Spanish for a single freckle. Luci took Kim to Texas after marrying Pat Nugent, but Freckles remained at the White House with the President. Him met his sad demise when a car ran over him while he was chasing a squirrel near the White House lawn.

After Him's death in 1966, J. Edgar Hoover, director of the Federal Bureau of Investigation and a former neighbor of President Johnson, gave the President yet another beagle, adding to the pack of presidential pets. The President named the dog J. Edgar but later dropped the initial and simply called the dog Edgar (the aforementioned victim of Blanco's nip).

Another addition to the Johnsons' animal kingdom came about by chance. While at a gas station in Austin on their way to the family ranch on Thanksgiving, Luci and her husband spotted a stray dog wandering around. Unable to locate its owner, the couple took him home. Luci named the dog Yuki, which means "snow" in Japanese. When Luci visited the President at the White House with Yuki, the President fell in love with the mutt, whose temperament and demeanor were charming. On the President's birthday in 1967, Luci told her father that he could keep Yuki. Clearly the President's favorite, Yuki was spotted with LBJ everywhere, including cabinet meetings, the signing of the Wholesome Meat Act, Lynda's wedding, and even the annual Christmas tree lighting ceremony, dressed in a dog-sized Santa suit. Yuki's favorite activity with the

**Left**
Lady Bird, LBJ, and Yuki relax near the Pedernales River at the LBJ Ranch, September 30, 1967.

President, however, was singing a duet while visitors to the Oval Office watched. The President once commented that Yuki was his favorite because "he speaks with a Texas accent."

Before leaving the White House, President and Mrs. Johnson gave Blanco to a doctor and his wife in Kentucky. Blanco died in September 1974 of a heart attack. Edgar moved to the Johnson family ranch. Yuki also returned to the ranch with President Johnson aboard Air Force One. When Johnson died of a heart attack in January 1973, Yuki was at his side. The dog then went to live with Luci and her family until his own death in 1979.

President Johnson's zeal for animals went beyond canines, however. As Traphes Bryant recalled, "Any man who felt about dogs the way he did would have won me over. And he didn't limit his enthusiasm just to dogs. When he drove around his ranch, an old buck deer he called George would sidle up to the car, and he would feed him through the window. He'd carry goodies in his pockets for everyone—candy for kids, lapel pins for men, Unipets (flavored vitamin treats) for dogs, sugar cubes for horses, deer, and mules. President Johnson was the greatest pet lover I have ever known—and possibly the greatest pet lover of all presidents. True, George Washington pampered his horses, President Jefferson trained a mockingbird to sit on his shoulder while he worked and also to meow like a cat, and President Harding taught his dog to sit on a chair and attend cabinet meetings. But they were pikers compared with President Johnson. Animals for LBJ were a way of life, sometimes an exotic one."

# The

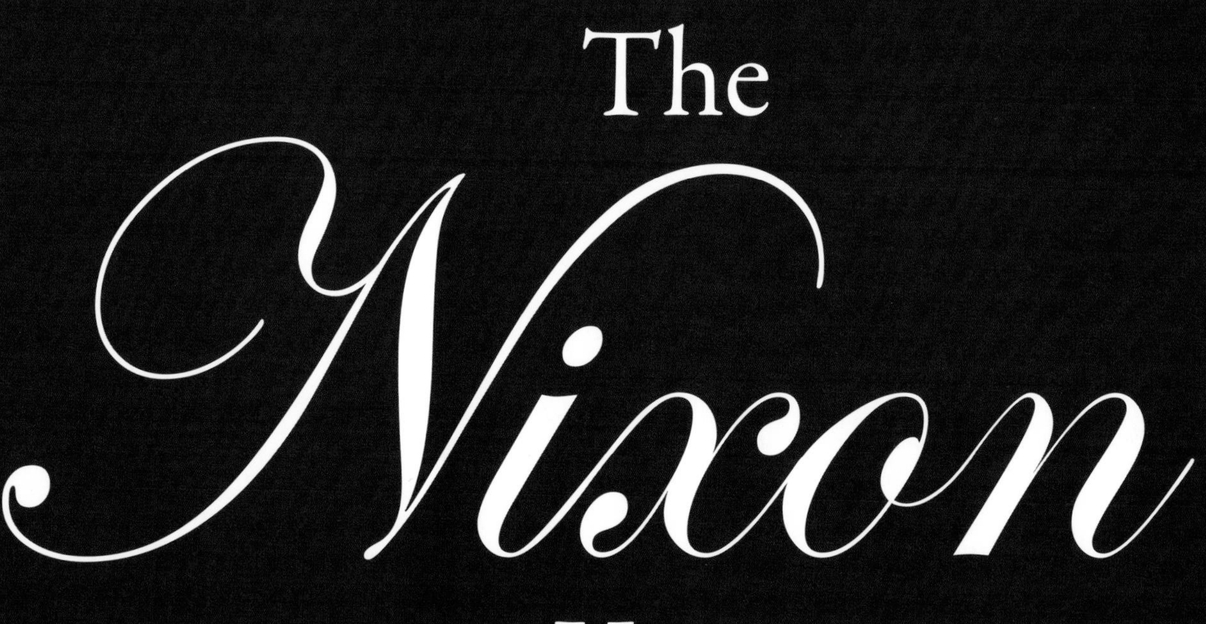


# Years

## 1969–1974

**VICKI ★ PASHA ★ KING TIMAHOE**

**President Richard Nixon**, along with First Lady Patricia Nixon, moved into the White House on January 20, 1969, with two dogs that belonged to their daughters, Julie and Tricia. His staff gave him another dog during the first few days of his presidency, but his most famous and remembered canine companion was the black-and-white cocker spaniel Checkers, who, incidentally, never lived in the White House.

The charming Checkers had been a steadfast playmate of the Nixon girls in their younger years. Even though he was a mere memory of the American public by the time President Nixon arrived at 1600 Pennsylvania Avenue, the little pup holds a permanent place in the hearts of dog lovers and historians alike, and his presence was well-noted early in the politician's career.

Nixon was the vice presidential candidate on the 1952 ticket (under presidential candidate Dwight D. Eisenhower) when a story broke, claiming that campaign donors were buying influence with Nixon by providing him with a secret cash fund for his personal expenses. Nixon responded to the claim, stating that the fund was not secret and that the campaign had commissioned an independent review, which revealed that the funds were used only for political purposes. Still, there was looming pressure for Eisenhower to remove his running mate from the ticket. Eisenhower, however, knew he needed to keep Nixon on to win, and on September 23, 1952, Nixon appeared on national television and delivered a half-hour address defending himself against the allegations, attacking his opponents, and urging the Republican National Committee to decide his fate. He revealed in detail his personal finances and mentioned the independent third-party review. It would mark the first time that a national political figure would release his tax returns. Ultimately, what people will always remember from the speech was not so much those details, but the mention of the one gift that he would keep and not give back: his daughters' cocker spaniel, Checkers.

"One other thing I probably should tell you because if we don't they'll probably be saying this about me, too, we did get something—a gift—after the [Senate] election. A man down in Texas heard Pat on the radio mention the fact that our two youngsters would like to have a dog. And, believe it or not, the day before we left on this campaign trip we got a message from Union Station in Baltimore saying they had a package for us. We went down to get it. You know what it was? It was a little cocker spaniel dog in a crate that he'd sent all the way from Texas. Black-and-white spotted. And our little girl—Tricia, the 6-year-old—named it Checkers. And you know, the kids, like all kids, love the dog and I just want to say this right now, that regardless of what they say about it, we're gonna keep it."

Approximately 60 million Americans heard the comeback speech of 1952, now commonly referred to as the Checkers Speech. The heartfelt address generated a groundswell of support from the base of the Republican camp and the general public, and the Eisenhower-Nixon ticket went on to win the election by 7 million votes. Checkers died years later, in the fall of 1964.

"Our dogs were treasured family members. Their charming ways and uncomplicated affection brought a special joy to each day in the White House."

Tricia Nixon Cox

Patricia Nixon Cox
DAUGHTER OF PRESIDENT AND MRS. NIXON

When the Nixons entered the White House, the two First Dogs were Julie's French poodle, Vicky, and Tricia's Yorkshire terrier, Pasha. On President Nixon's 65th birthday, January 9, 1969, just days before he took the oath of office, his personal staff from the campaign gave him a small model of an Irish setter—a representation of the dog that was to come. President-Elect Nixon announced that day that he wanted to meet the dog to "judge his personality" before naming him, but that it would certainly be given a good Irish name. The Nixons were thrilled to be receiving an Irish setter and had fond memories of the breed, because they had one as a pet many years earlier. On January 28, the President received his actual gift in the Rose Garden at the White House. He named the Irish setter King Timahoe, or Tim, as he was often affectionately called, after the small village in Ireland where Nixon's mother's Quaker ancestors came from.

Nixon did receive two other famous gifts during his tenure as President: giant pandas. Chairman Mao Zedong of the People's Republic of China gave pandas Ling-Ling and Hsing-Hsing to President Nixon in 1972 after his historic visit to the country. (Nixon responded by sending Zedong a pair of musk oxen.) Twenty thousand people visited the pandas the first day they were on display at the National Zoo in Washington, D.C., and an additional estimated 1 million visitors came to see them that first year. The pandas were wildly popular, and China's gift was seen as an enormous diplomatic success.

Despite the great exotic gift, Nixon preferred his canine companions. White House staff electrician Trophes Bryant, the unofficial keeper of the presidential kennels, recalled the immense joy President Nixon received from watching his dogs. "For daily relaxation, the new President really got his biggest kick out of watching King Tim—especially watching him point.

**Preceding Pages**
President Nixon in the White House Rose Garden welcoming King Timahoe, a birthday present from his senior staff.

King Timahoe enjoying the fountain on the South Lawn.

**Opposite**
Pasha, Vicky, and Tim posing for the cameras.

**Left**
The entire Nixon clan—including Pasha, Vicky, and Tim—gather around the Christmas tree in the private residence of the White House during a taping for CBS.

I will never forget this [one] particular day, because Nixon stood absolutely motionless for fully 10 minutes as Tim stood riveted, pointing at a bird in a tree, nose stretched outward, one paw raised off the ground, tail straight out, and body leaning forward. It was the bird that finally tired of the game and flew away."

The sheer pleasure of observing his dogs was a ritual Nixon continued throughout his days at the White House. Later in the administration he often dined on the Truman balcony, requesting that the dogs be let out on the South Lawn to play so that he could watch them while he ate. He even kept a stash of dog biscuits in his desk drawer in the Oval Office.

The Nixon family very much believed in spoiling their pets. Every year at Christmas, Mrs. Nixon made sure there was a tree upstairs in the private residence of the White House specifically for the Nixon dogs. The dog run, located behind the West Wing, included a heated doghouse, complete with three suites, where the canines spent much of their time. It, too, was decorated for the holidays. The three dogs romped around the South Lawn twice a day, weather permitting, and when it was too cold for them to be out, they were cozily secured in a storeroom.

One of Patricia Nixon Cox's favorite memories of the dogs at the White House was on the day of her wedding. As she and her father were walking down the steps of the South Portico, her father pointed out the trio. She couldn't believe her eyes—each dog sported a collar of flowers, specially commissioned by the First Couple. The three canines sat ceremoniously still, honoring the First Daughter's big occasion.

All three dogs were, reportedly, perfectly behaved while living at the Executive Mansion. They all wore modest red collars and had matching red leashes. Tim had dog license No. 1, Pasha had No. 2, and Vicky No. 3, and each had its own unique personality. Tim

**Opposite**
President and Mrs. Nixon walking the dogs at Camp David in 1972—all outfitted in holiday attire.

**Left**
The President (in California) gazes affectionately as Tim makes himself couch-comfortable, July 8, 1972.

was known to welcome all guests into the White House, and during his days at 1600 he became famous for greeting visitors with a polite paw-shake. It became a ritual of sorts for foreign dignitaries to be photographed shaking hands with Tim. Pasha was his inseparable playmate, and President Nixon liked to say that the Yorkshire was his special connection to the people of England. Vicky, the poodle, seized every opportunity to chase the goldfish (occasionally savoring one for dinner) in the small fishpond Lady Bird Johnson had installed on the South Grounds. Unfortunately for Pasha, she was too small to join in and would sit and bark in frustration.

The Nixons' dogs were popular during all of their years at the White House, and press photos appeared frequently in newspapers and magazines. One particular media favorite was a photo of the dogs in front of their Christmas tree. The second most-requested photo given out by the Nixon White House (the top choice being one of the President himself) was an image of the three Nixon dogs sitting in front of the White House on the South Lawn. All three dogs joined the President when he left office.

# The

# Ford

# Years

1974–1977

LIBERTY ★ MISTY ★ SHAN

**President Gerald Ford** was among the few to assume the Office of President of the United States without spending years seeking it. He was truly the man next door. This perception was personified not only by Ford while he lived in the White House, but also by his entire family throughout his administration. Ford came to 1600 Pennsylvania Avenue on August 9, 1974, with his wife, Betty; their youngest child, Susan; and Susan's Siamese cat, Shan Shein. They did not have a dog, but that quickly changed.

President and Mrs. Ford had several dogs together before they acquired a golden retriever named Liberty. In 1955 Gerald Ford's college roommate and godfather to his son Jack gave the family a golden retriever named Brown Sugar. He was a close member of the family and lived with them for 13 years. Following Brown Sugar's death, the Fords acquired another retriever they named Sugar, who sadly passed away shortly before Ford became Vice President. Life in the First Residence without a dog was a situation Susan was determined to amend.

Just weeks after the family moved into the White House, First Lady Betty Ford underwent a mastectomy for breast cancer. It was a difficult time not only for her but also for the President, who was caring for his beloved wife during her recovery while facing another daunting task—trying to restore the country's faith in the government following the resignation of President Richard Nixon. Susan, along with family friend and photographer David Kennerly, conspired to brighten everyone's spirits, thinking that a golden retriever puppy would surely do the trick. President Ford later recounted Liberty's arrival at the White House in his memoir *A Time To Heal*: "Our family didn't have a dog when we moved into the White House. Susan and David [Kennerly, the White House photographer] thought that situation should be rectified before Betty came home from the hospital. Without telling me his intention, David did some research and discovered that a fine retriever had recently given birth to a litter in Minneapolis. [The breeder of the dark gold pup was Avis Friberg of Excelsior, Minnesota.] David called the kennel's owner and said he wanted to buy a puppy for a friend. That was fine, the owner said, but what was the name of David's friend? David said it was a surprise; he wanted to keep the name secret. 'We don't sell dogs that way,' the owner replied. 'We have to know if the dog is going to a good home.' 'The couple is friendly,' David assured him. 'They're middle-aged, and they live in a white house with a big yard and a fence around it. It's a lovely place.' 'Do they own or rent?' the owner asked. David thought for a minute. 'I guess you might call it public housing,' he said. The owner said the dog was healthy, and that she was going to eat a lot. Did his friend have a steady job? David could play the game no longer. He hinted that his friend was a very important person and finally the owner agreed to fly the dog to Washington. I was in the Oval Office

"Liberty was Jerry's favorite advisor.
She gave him something no one
else could share."

Betty Ford

**Preceding Pages**
President and Mrs. Ford pose with Liberty on the South Lawn of the White House.

President Ford confides in Liberty at Camp David following a campaign strategy meeting, August 7, 1976.

**Above**
Liberty in the Oval Office.

**Right**
President and Mrs. Ford with Susan and Liberty at Camp David, August 7, 1976.

**Left**
Gerald R. Ford poses with his sons Steve, Jack, and Mike and their golden retriever, Brown Sugar, in the backyard of the family residence in Alexandria, Virginia, December 1972.

the day before Betty came back from the hospital when Susan walked in. 'Daddy,' she asked, 'if we ever get another dog, what kind are we going to get?' 'A female golden retriever about 6 months old,' I said. At that moment, David entered with a copper-colored pup who raced around the Oval Office yelping excitedly. 'Whose dog is that?' I asked. 'It's yours.' Susan and David laughed. 'Her name was Streaker, but we've changed it to Liberty.' Delighted, I grabbed the pup, put her on my lap, then got down on my hands and knees and played with her on the rug. That was a joyous experience, and I knew that Betty would be just as thrilled as I was to welcome the new addition to our family."

Liberty was instantly embraced by the entire family and quickly became a darling of the media. She licked Mrs. Ford on the face the minute they met on the South Lawn upon her arrival back to the White House from the hospital. On October 9, 1974, President Ford even referenced Liberty in a speech he made in Philadelphia: "In the appropriate spirit of the city of Philadelphia, we have named her Liberty. One of those inquisitive reporters that we have in Washington asked Susan who is going to take care of Liberty; who is going to feed her and groom her and take her out each night or every morning? And Susan did not hesitate one minute. She said, 'Of course, it will be Dad.' So, I have this feeling—this is one Liberty that is going to cost me some of mine. But in a very broader sense, that is the true nature of liberty. It comes with both privileges and obligations. Freedom, we all know, is seldom free."

Liberty quickly made the White House her home and seemed to know no boundaries within it. She was often found in the Oval Office, where she would stand by the door when she wanted to be let out. Mrs. Ford described her, saying, "Liberty was always a lady. She was well-trained." However, a favorite story from the Ford Administration demonstrated the sincere character of the President and involved a very young Liberty. Members of the administration recall how Mr. Ford treated people, regarless of their stations in life, with dignity and respect. They often tell of the day when the President's dog soiled the carpet in the Oval Office and a Navy steward scrambled to clean it. The President stopped him, stating, "I'll do that. No man should have to clean up after another man's dog."

There were occasional comments in the paper or observations by the press, however, questioning the conviviality between Liberty and Shan, Susan's cat. (Shan was named after a village in China the family visited while Ford was a congressman.) The petite seal point Siamese, who had been an Easter present for Susan, resided in the First Daughter's

VH-3A
150616
DANGER
KEEP AWAY

**Left**
President Ford, along with Chief of Staff Don Rumsfeld, daughter Susan, Army Aide Major Robert E. Barrett, a Secret Service agent, and Liberty, walk across the South Lawn to Marine One, which took them to Andrews Air Force Base, — October 7, 1974.

**Opposite**
Liberty jumping over the hedges outside the Oval Office along the West Colonnade.

**Left**
The Ford family on the White House grounds: (left to right) Susan, Mike, Gayle, President and Mrs. Ford with Liberty, Jack, and Steve, September 6, 1976.

**Below**
Susan Ford with Shan, the Ford family's Siamese cat, October 4, 1974.

room on the third floor of the White House and slept on a heating pad, although it was also divulged that the cat pretty much had the run of the family quarters. When the press pool would ask White House press spokesmen about the Liberty-Shan relationship, they would receive replies such as, "Well, they get along fine for a dog and a cat." But Kennerly admitted the unfortunate truth. "No way. They do not get along," he said. "Shan hates Liberty." Liberty was known for charging upstairs to the family quarters and sniffing out Shan's cat food, which the dog liked.

So intriguing were the dog-and-cat calamities that Richard H. Growald, UPI senior editor, chronicled Shan's "predicament" in "Life Is Not Easy for White House Cat." "Shan tiptoes down the back stairs from the third floor, carefully using its cream-and-chocolate head around each corner to make sure Liberty and other alien beings are not around," Growald reported in the 1975 article.

He further noted, "Shan has a thing about men. And hates all but one man, the President. It rubs up against the President's feet and, Susan said, hops onto Ford's lap and allows him to pet it. But no other male, not even Secretary of State Henry Kissinger, has established any more of a détente with Shan than has Liberty. At the sight of a nonpresident male, or of Liberty, Shan dashes to its favorite hiding place, under the bed of the Lincoln bedroom, according to Kennerly."

**Left**
Liberty takes a dip in the South Lawn fountain, November 1974.

## TOO MUCH LIBERTY

The most amusing story of Liberty's White House days occurred while she was expecting. It was recounted in Mrs. Ford's memoir: "With motherhood imminent, we were afraid she'd deliver at night, so we moved her inside.... About three o'clock in the morning, she came and licked Jerry's face [needing to be let outside]. Like a good daddy, he got up, pulled on a robe and slippers, took the dog downstairs and out onto the South Lawn. When they were ready to come back, Jerry rang for the elevator. But at night the elevator goes off—you have to get it charged up or something. Secret Service agents are in a room in the basement (they have a mirror and closed-circuit TV and there are lights all over the grounds), and usually they notice anything that moves, so I still don't understand how they missed the scene with the odd couple. Maybe somebody dozed off. Anyway, Jerry decided to try the stairs. He opened the door to the stairwell, said, 'Come on, Liberty,' and up they climbed to the second floor, Liberty waddling from side to side, her stomach with nine puppies in it practically hanging on the ground. They got to the second floor, and the door to the hall was locked. You can get out, but you can't get back in. They went up again, to the third floor. Also locked. And there they were, a President and his dog, wandering around in a stairwell in the wee small hours of the morning, not able to get back to bed. Finally they came all the way down again, and by that time the Secret Service had been alerted, and somebody got the elevator started."

**Left**
First Lady Betty Ford and her golden retriever, Liberty, watch over Liberty's puppies on the South Lawn of the White House, October 5, 1975.

**Right**
Susan, Mrs. Ford, and President Ford with Liberty and her puppies, September 16, 1975.

**Below**
President Ford, Mrs. Ford, Steve, and Susan feed Flag the deer at Camp David, September 1, 1974.

**Opposite Top**
President Ford along with Lieutenant General Brent Scowcroft, assistant to the President for National Security Affairs, walks Liberty and Misty.

**Opposite Bottom**
President and Mrs. Ford and daughter Susan play with Liberty's puppies on the South Lawn of the White House, November 5, 1975.

The President may have won the cat's affections, but a running joke was that when Kennerly confided to the press that Ford was a dog man at heart, the statement may have cost the President the cat lovers' vote.

Rivalries aside, the Fords were animal lovers with a "more the merrier" mind-set, and in 1975 they decided to breed Liberty. So while the family vacationed that summer in Vail, Colorado, Liberty went to Medford, Oregon, to spend some time with Misty Sun Gold Ladd, known as Ladd—a champion of sorts, who belonged to a breeder referred by the kennel that sold Liberty. Ladd had already sired more than 400 pups. The media went crazy over Liberty and her prospective offspring, and the number of the United Airlines flight she took to Oregon—to meet her likely suitor—was even leaked to the press. Despite the frenzy, the dogs' encounter was a success.

The White House was not originally set up for a dog to give birth, but Mrs. Ford created cozy-yet-practical accommodations. She emptied a small room on the family floor of the Executive Mansion and lined it with canvas and plastic. It was, as some newspapers

**Right**
President and Mrs. Ford with Liberty and Misty and their puppies. This was the photo for their 1977 Christmas card.

**Opposite**
Susan and Liberty watch as Marine One departs the White House with President Ford.

reported, "where many of the 10 daily newspapers the President receives undoubtedly will be put to good use." White House carpenters and part of the Executive Residence staff helped build a whelping box for Liberty, so she had her own little "hospital," as Mrs. Ford described it. Liberty gave birth on September 14, 1975, to four females and five males. The First Lady sat with Liberty and stroked her head for eight hours before the first puppy arrived, and continued to stay, holding Liberty's head, while Susan and the vet attended to Liberty and the rest of the puppies. The litter contained only one blonde, and Mrs. Ford decided that would be the one they kept. She named her Misty. Later she wrote: "Sometimes I feel guilty because Misty grew into a big, strong, husky animal who ought to be a working dog, not just a house pet, but I don't think I could part with her now."

On September 15, White House Press Representative Bill Greener made the first official press statement about the puppies: "The President and Mrs. Ford are pleased to announce the birth of the ninetuplets to their close personal friend and houseguest, Liberty. The First Dog went into labor shortly after noon on Sunday. The first puppy was born at 12:30; the ninth puppy was born at 8:17 p.m." When the press asked about the father, he wittily replied, "The father is proud. As most of you know, the proud father is Misty Sun Gold Ladd. He is a 10-year-old golden retriever from Medford, Oregon, and I am told he has 400 other children by previous marriages."

Mrs. Ford was very protective of the pups. Out of concern for their eyes, she did not allow a photo of the pups to be taken until they were two months old. David Kennerly took the first photo, and it was a laborious session. Trying to get all nine puppies artistically arranged was nearly impossible; every time they thought they were perfectly posed, one would wander off. Mrs. Ford was also very protective of their lungs. She hung a sign over the door to the puppies' room that read "NO SMOKING, AND THIS MEANS YOU GRANDPA." This cautionary note included a sketch of President Ford with his pipe.

Everyone in the country wanted one of the presidential pups. Letters flowed into the White House, some including endorsements and recommendations from senators, including Senator Bob Dole. President and Mrs. Ford gave one of the puppies—which was named Jerry—to the Leader Dog School for the Blind. Four others went to friends, and other friends bought the last three for $300 each to cover the cost of breeding Liberty.

During her days as First Dog, Liberty was a superstar in her own right. She won distinctions and honors, including the Top Dog Award presented by the Michigan Humane Society in recognition of outstanding service on behalf of kindness to all her fellow canines. Stories indicate that if President Ford wanted to end a conversation in the Oval Office, he would signal Liberty and she would go to the guest wagging her tail, creating a natural break. Even photographs of the dog were autographed with a rubber stamp of her paw print. When President and Mrs. Ford left the White House, Liberty and Misty went with them and were featured in their 1977 Christmas card, each with a new litter of puppies. Liberty passed away at the age of 11 in 1986. Susan Ford currently has three golden retrievers.

# The Carter Years

1977–1981

MISTY MALARKY YING YANG ★ GRITS

**President Jimmy Carter** took the oath of office on January 20, 1977, to become the 39th President of the United States. He grew up in Plains, Georgia, where, as a boy, he had a pet dog named Bozo and a horse named Lady Lee. President Carter moved into the White House with First Lady Rosalynn Carter; their young daughter, Amy; and her Siamese cat, Misty Malarky Ying Yang. Misty, as he was affectionately called, remained with the family in the First Residence throughout the President's tenure and was the last cat to occupy the White House until President Bill Clinton moved in with his cat, Socks, in 1993.

When the Carter family entered the White House, their three eldest children, Jack, Chip, and Jeff, were already grown, so Amy, who was 9 years old when the family moved to D.C., was the only Carter child to live at 1600 Pennsylvania Avenue. However, with her brown-and-black Siamese cat by her side, the First Daughter was far from lonely. The cat was a constant companion to Amy and lived with her in the private residence of the White House on the second floor.

Not long after the family settled in, her fourth-grade teacher, Mrs. Verona Meeder, gave Amy the gift of a black-and-white border collie puppy. Amy named the dog Grits—a fitting Southern name for a Georgia family pet. Unfortunately, the puppy didn't stay long at the White House—it was rumored that Misty was not a big fan of Grits—but before his departure he did participate in one official White House event: Heartworm Awareness Week, created to educate people about the preventable disease. Grits was ultimately returned to the teacher. The animal gifts did not stop with a dog, however. A Sri Lanka elephant was given to the Carters. Too large for the White House, it, of course, went to live at the National Zoo.

Just as the public—and the press—clamored for details about the First Family, they were also curious about what life in the White House was like for the cunning cat. Misty rarely left the mansion, preferring to stay snug in the family quarters with his young mistress, although he once flew with Amy on the presidential helicopter. On another occasion, he was allowed to mingle with the outside world and gave an exclusive "interview" to *The Christian Science Monitor*—not exactly a tell-all, purr se, but it was revealing, at least for those interested in the topics of mice, visiting dignitaries, and the feline's own royal ancestry. Headlined "First Cat Denies Rise in Mice," the piece was a cheeky rebuttal to reports in *The Washington Star* that claimed that mice had been found everywhere in the White House, from the Oval Office to the flowerpots of the East Wing. Misty denied the allegations, appearing, according to *The Christian Science Monitor*, "poised and confident, his dark brown mask grave and his blue eyes confident as he fielded questions from the floor."

The 2-year-old cat went on to discuss his appearance at a state dinner for Mexican President Lopez Portillo. In her autobiography, the First Lady recounted a funny incident from that dinner, just as she and the President were asked to walk down the grand stairway. "Drawing a deep breath, I moved with Jimmy to the top of the

"Misty, my cat, was one of my best friends and she really turned the White House into a home."

Amy Carter
DAUGHTER OF PRESIDENT AND MRS. CARTER

**Preceding Pages**
Amy Carter takes a portrait with her Siamese cat, Misty Malarky Ying Yang, August 15, 1977.

President Carter and daughter Amy, with their new dog, Grits, a gift to Amy from her school teacher, on the South Lawn of the White House, June 9, 1977.

**Right**
Jimmy Carter as a child with his dog Bozo, 1937.

**Opposite**
Amy Carter with Grits on the steps of the White House, 1977.

grand stairway. The Marine Band announcing us blared forth, the military aides snapped to attention, and at the foot of the stairs the guests and a battery of press waited expectantly in this very formal atmosphere. First down the stairs in the spotlight the whole way padded Misty Malarky! I don't know who was more surprised—the guests, the press, me, or Misty. But immediately there was laughter in the great hallway, and a relaxed and comfortable, warm, elegant, and thrilling evening had begun."

When asked about the delicate issue of a White House sandbox, *The Christian Science Monitor* reported that "Yang twitched his whiskers and growled, 'no comment.'" When asked by a *Monitor* reporter if he'd consider endorsing a product, as some of his contemporaries had done, he first refused to dignify the question with a reply, but then went on to answer, before stalking off: "Those of us with breeding," he said, alluding to his Siamese ancestors, "do not use our high government connections to endorse commercial products." Though later, in 1986, after the First Family had returned to Georgia, Misty appeared inside and on the cover of the 1986 Purina Cat Chow celebrity cat calendar, which also included Elizabeth Taylor's cat Cleo and Andy Warhol's cat Katie. It was never revealed whether Misty actually ate Purina Cat Chow. The cat left the White House with the Carter family in 1981.

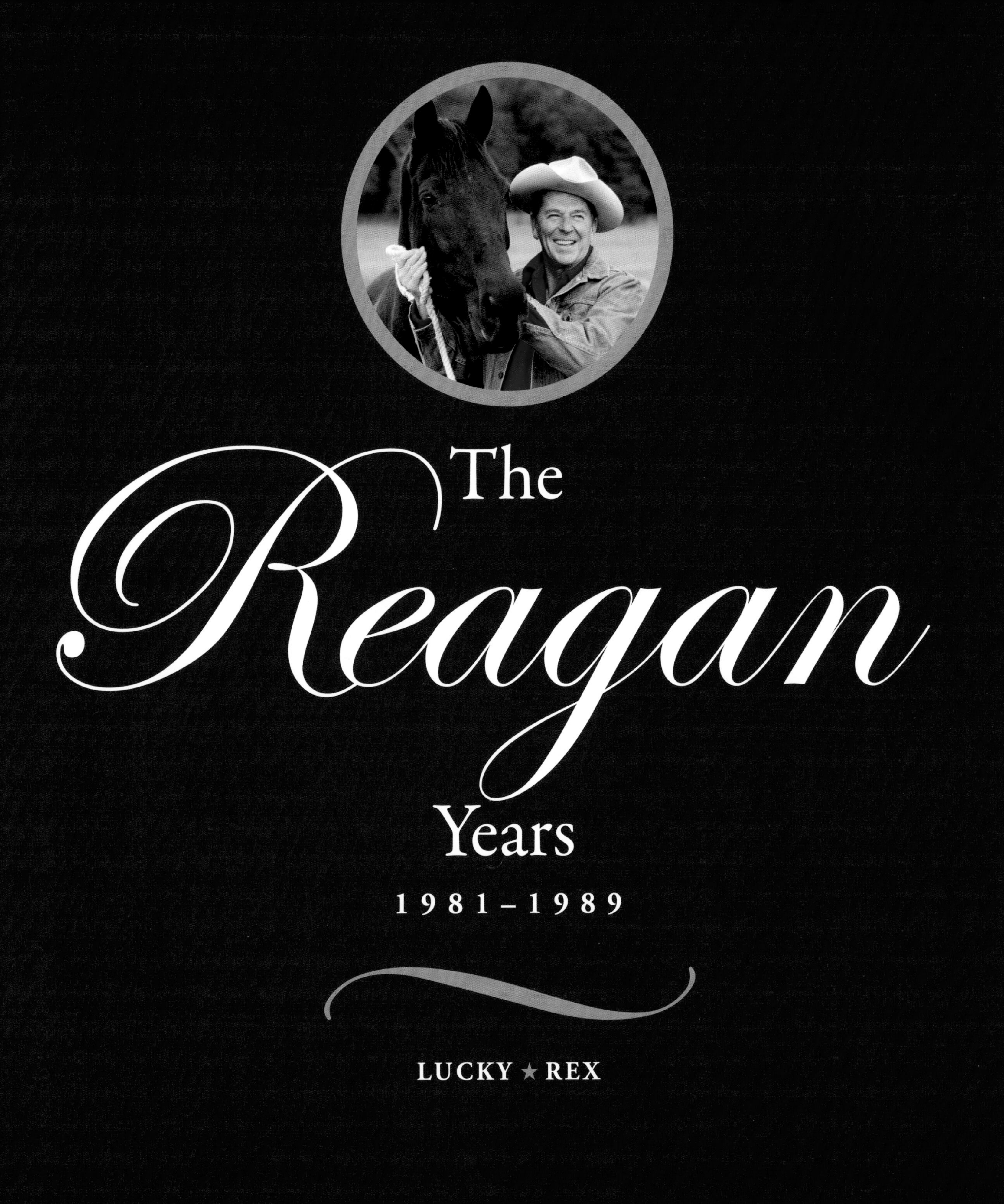

# The Reagan Years

1981–1989

LUCKY ★ REX

**President Ronald Reagan**, the 40th President of the United States of America, entered the White House in 1981 with his beloved wife, Nancy. Both were well-known animal lovers. The First Couple's menagerie comprised everything from goldfish to cows, and they had four dogs and five horses at the time he was elected to office. Despite the First Couple's abundant affection for their pets, they were kept at Rancho del Cielo, the President's Santa Barbara, California, ranch known as the Western White House, so there were no household pets at 1600 Pennsylvania Avenue during Reagan's first term. However, a little girl from Kentucky changed that, and during his second term two new dogs called the White House home.

Rancho del Cielo, also known as Sky's Ranch or Heaven's Ranch, is a 688-acre spread located on the top of the Santa Ynez Mountain range northwest of Santa Barbara, California. It was a vacation home for the Reagans and a permanent haven for their animals. During his presidency, Reagan enjoyed many much-needed retreats at the ranch, where he reconnected with the dogs, horses, and longhorn steers. The four-legged family grew in number throughout his two terms. The resident ranch dogs were Taca, a husky; Millie, a black Labrador retriever; Victory, a golden retriever given to the President in 1980 in Wisconsin while he campaigned there; and Freebo, a mutt that belonged to his daughter Patti Davis. The horses were No Strings and Dormita, both quarter horses; Gwalianko, El Alamein, El Saraf, and Catalina, all Arabians; and El Primero Tentiente (translation: first lieutenant), a Peruvian Paso (a breed of saddle horse known for its smooth ride). The horses were allowed to run freely and were stabled only for feeding. The Reagans almost always rode while at the ranch, especially in the morning, and the dogs usually followed close behind.

Four years after he took the oath of office—following a historic landslide reelection—President and Mrs. Reagan welcomed a dog to live with them in the Executive Mansion. On December 6, 1984, just after the Thanksgiving holiday, a 9-week-old Bouvier des Flandres became First Pup. They called the young dog Lucky, a nod to Mrs. Reagan's mother, Edith Luckett Davis. Lucky was presented to the First Lady by 1985 March of Dimes poster child Kristen Ellis of Kentucky and was much loved by everyone at the White House and across the country. As Donald Regan, the President's chief of staff, recalled, "Lucky dropped by my office for a doughnut every morning before galloping thunderously back to the residence." Ralston-Purina wanted to launch a new line of dog food in honor of the First Pup and offered the President and First Lady a free lifetime supply, but the First Couple declined. They did, however, concede to allow Lucky to do the official tasting. The pup's popularity soared,

SEAL OF THE PRESIDENT OF THE UNITED STATES

"Our dogs were always part of our family, whether sleeping in our beds on rainy nights or hanging out in the Oval Office years later. My father always undertook the task of dog training himself, and every one of our dogs looked to him as their master."

Patti Davis

Patti Davis
DAUGHTER OF PRESIDENT AND MRS. REAGAN

**Preceding Pages**
The President and First Lady take a relaxing stroll with Lucky at Camp David, May 18, 1985.

**Opposite**
President Reagan visits with Lucky in the West Colonnade, May 31, 1985.

**Left**
Mrs. Reagan bathes and grooms Lucky, April 1, 1985.

and the nation's schoolchildren sent a lot of fan mail to the pooch. A White House correspondent sent back signed photographs of Lucky. As the dog's popularity increased, so did her size, and in her first year she grew to be more than 2 feet tall and 80 pounds—a bit daunting for the Reagan White House. The Reagans sent her to obedience school for five weeks, with hopes of shaping her into a more manageable pet but ultimately decided she'd be happier where she could roam free. Mrs. Reagan described Lucky's move in her memoirs: "She was just a little bundle of fur when I got her, but she grew to be the size of a pony. When she became too big for the White House, we took her to live at the ranch, with the other four dogs. She's in heaven."

Soon after Lucky's departure, a 1-year-old male Cavalier King Charles spaniel named Rex came to live at the First Residence. He was an early Christmas gift to Nancy from the President, who adopted the dog from William F. Buckley (who owned Rex's brother Fred), a well-known commentator and good friend of the President. He was named for Rex Scouten, the White House chief usher who retired in 1985. One of Rex's first official gestures was to help throw the switch that lit the National Christmas Tree. Rex had his own doghouse, designed by Theo Hayes, the great-great grandson of former President Rutherford B. Hayes. Decorated in high style, it featured framed portraits of the President and First Lady and red curtains. But at night, Rex slept just across the hall from the President's bedroom in a basket in the kitchen. And Mrs. Reagan once noted, "By the time the papers arrived we'd be sharing the bed with Rex." More than just a friend, Rex became a political asset for the President, adeptly helping him dodge questions from the press. Once, in 1986, Reagan was heading off to a weekend at Camp David when reporters confronted him, shouting inquisitions about threats from Libyan leader Muammar Gaddafi. The President grinned and pointed to the brown-and-white spaniel straining at the end of his leash. "Guard dog!" Reagan declared.

Historians have explored various tales surrounding the ghost of Abe Lincoln, most of them involving sightings in the Lincoln Bedroom. Rex apparently subscribed to these bits of folklore, as President Reagan recounted in his autobiography, *An American Life*: "We'd [President and Mrs. Reagan] heard the legend that Lincoln's ghost haunted parts of the second floor and took it all with a grain of salt. Then something happened involving our dog, Rex, that nearly made me join the believers. One night, we were sitting in the

**Right**
President Reagan and Prime Minister Margaret Thatcher walk Lucky in the White House Rose Garden, February 20, 1985.

**Above**
The President and First Lady ride horses at Rancho Del Cielo (the Western White House), April 8, 1985.

**Right**
President Reagan, at Rancho Del Cielo, tends to one of his cherished horses, July 3, 1982.

**Opposite**
The First Couple on Thanksgiving holiday at their ranch getaway, November 24, 1981.

living room of the family quarters when Rex suddenly started down the length of the Central Hall toward the other end of the building. His eyes were fixed straight ahead, and his ears stood up as straight as two flagpoles. I looked out and couldn't see anything. Rex started barking loudly and edging slowly down the hall. … He got as far as the door [to the bedroom] and stopped; he stopped barking and, with a deep growl, started backing away from the door and would not go in. Finally he just ran away from whatever it was that had scared him."

Both Lucky and Rex led active lives during their White House days, participating in many of the President's and First Lady's daily activities. They especially loved going to Camp David. The First Lady described how much the dogs enjoyed the lifts from the South Lawn. "I was never crazy about the helicopter, although as helicopters go, ours was large, and the ride was fairly smooth. I'm sure one image that people will always remember of the Reagan years is of Ronnie and me leaving the South Lawn of the White House for Camp David. Sam Donaldson would be shouting something to Ronnie, who could rarely hear

**Opposite**
The Reagans at Camp David in Maryland, July 21, 1984.

**Left**
President and Mrs. Reagan with Rex during an interview with Barbara Walters, February 25, 1986.

**Below**
The President and First Lady with Lucky and their cats at Rancho Del Cielo, August 23, 1986.

**Preceding Pages**
President and Mrs. Reagan with First Dog Rex at the National Christmas Tree lighting ceremony, December 12, 1985.

President Reagan walking with Don Regan and Lucky down the West Colonnade, July 10, 1985.

**Above**
President and Mrs. Reagan with Rex arrive home at the White House via Marine One, April 20, 1987.

**Oppposite**
"Window, please!" President Reagan and Lucky take in the view from Marine One, November 1, 1985.

him over the noise of the helicopter's engine. I would be walking behind Ronnie, led by one of the dogs—either Lucky, until she became too big to live at the White House, or Rex. ... Both dogs loved to ride in the helicopter; they knew we were headed for Camp David, where they had room to run around. During the flight, they would sit peacefully and look out the window. Lucky usually sat on Ronnie's lap."

Rex lived at the White House until the end of Reagan's last term. In January 1989, just a few days before the President's departure and George Bush's inauguration, White House staffers gave the departing Reagans farewell gifts, including a replica of the White House for Rex. "He's already taken over this White House," the President told the crowd at the gathering. "I'm glad he's got one of his own now. And you know something? He doesn't get kicked out of it after two terms." Rex moved with President and Mrs. Reagan to their new home in Los Angeles and lived to be 13.

Reagan passed on his fondness for animals to his children, and at the President's funeral, Patti recalled her father's compassion. "He was the one who generously offered funeral services for my goldfish on the morning of its demise. We went out into the garden, and we dug a tiny grave with a teaspoon and he took two twigs and lashed them together with twine and formed a cross as a marker for the grave. And then he gave a beautiful eulogy. He told me that my fish was swimming in the clear blue waters in heaven and he would never tire and he would never get hungry and he would never be in any danger and he could swim as far and wide as he wanted and he never had to stop, because the river went on forever. He was free. When we went back inside and I looked at my remaining goldfish in their aquarium with their pink plastic castle and their colored rocks, I suggested that perhaps we should kill the others so they could also go to that clear blue river and be free. He then took more time out of this morning—I'm sure

**Right**
President Reagan rides El Alamein, his favorite horse, at Rancho Del Cielo (the Western White House) as Victory and Freebo follow close behind, April 4, 1986.

**Below**
President Reagan plays with Victory (near Marine One) at Rancho Del Cielo, August 6, 1981.

he actually did have other things to do that day—and patiently explained to me that in God's time, the other fish would go there, as well. In God's time, we would all be taken home. And even though it sometimes seemed a mystery, we were just asked to trust that God's time was right and wise."

Reagan once said of his beloved California ranch, "No place before or since has ever given Nancy and me the joy and serenity it does." Perhaps no other place is as revealing of Ronald Reagan's character and heart as Rancho del Cielo's Boot Hill. Many of the President's dogs, some horses, and livestock were laid to rest in this spot, memorialized with headstones into which he personally and painstakingly carved their names. Both Rex and Lucky, along with many other Reagan pets, including Old Duke and the First Lady's favorite horse, No Strings, are buried there.

# The *Bush* Years

1989–1993

MILLIE ★ RANGER

**President George H. W. Bush** and First Lady Barbara Bush, well-known pet lovers throughout their lives, were the proud owners of Mildred Kerr Bush—fondly and famously called Millie—when they entered the White House. Millie became a household name and was simply the most famous dog in White House history. The brown-and-white springer spaniel was celebrated by the nation and even "wrote" a best-selling book, *Millie's Book: As Dictated to Barbara Bush.*

President and Mrs. Bush's reputation as pet lovers was cemented long before they arrived at 1600 Pennsylvania Avenue. Millie was only partly responsible, as there were other animals that preceded her. As a child, Barbara Bush had a cairn terrier named Sandy, and she and President Bush loved and cared for many dogs over the years, including a black poodle named Turbo, a brown mutt named Cosy, a white collie named Gaines' Markham or "Mark," a white poodle named Nicky, and a black miniature poodle named Motsy.

As the First Lady once commented in an interview, "All the time our children were growing up, we owned dogs. I think they teach children responsibility. And in our world it is nice for children to have something warm and furry to come home to."

Before Millie there was the incomparable C. Fred. The couple's son Marvin and good friend Don Rhodes gave Mrs. Bush the golden cocker spaniel as a birthday gift. Mrs. Bush described that day: "In June, on my 48th birthday, the family surprised me with a 2-month-old blond cocker spaniel. After much thought, we named the puppy after C. Fred Chambers, a dear friend of George's. … I really needed a dog. It was Marvin's idea, and George asked our friend Don Rhodes to take him dog shopping. Don said Marvin looked deeply into the eyes of dozens of dogs until he finally found the perfect pup—C. Fred. It was an absolutely perfect birthday present."

This marked the Bushes' first claim to national dog-loving fame. C. Fred immediately was embraced as part of the family, and the dog moved with them around the globe as Mr. Bush's career dictated, including a stint in China while he was an ambassador. It was not the original plan for C. Fred to accompany the Bushes overseas. But it was just a year after Mrs. Bush received him, and she was determined that he go.

"[After] George had broken the news to me that C. Fred could not go to China, I asked the State Department people, and they said there were American dogs in China. Then I asked the Chinese, and they said there were many foreign dogs there. That settled it: C. Fred was going! I shipped 17 cases of his special food, so then George had to let him go; he had too big an investment in dog food not to. We never regretted taking him. There were lonely times, and both George and I enjoyed curling up with a good book and C. Fred at our side."

Friends also spent time with the Bushes while they were living in Beijing, and visitors were warned of C.

**Preceding Page**
President and Mrs. Bush with C. Fred on the rocks at Walker's Point, Kennebunkport, Maine, September 3, 1982.

**Right**
Margaret Thatcher (with Mrs. Bush) gives her regards to C. Fred at the Vice President's Residence on the grounds of the U.S. Naval Observatory in Washington, D.C.

**Left**
C. Fred in front of the Vice President's (and his own) Residence.

**Below**
A young President and Mrs. Bush with C. Fred.

Fred's favorite "toys." As it turned out, his favorite playthings were guests' personal items. Notes were placed in visitors' rooms, cautioning: "Beware of the Bush Dragon. He eats socks, furs, gloves, and slippers. Please keep your doors closed, or put your things up high. His name is C. Fred."

C. Fred returned to the States with the Bushes and eventually appeared on magazine covers. He was loved by the media and wildly popular, especially while Mr. Bush was Vice President. It was during that time the book *C. Fred's Story*, "edited slightly" by Barbara Bush, was released. The book's proceeds benefited a literary charity, a favorite cause of Mrs. Bush.

C. Fred passed away in January 1987. Following his death, Vice President Bush approached good friends Sarah and Will Farish about their black-and-white springer spaniels, a mother-and-daughter pair that had, weeks earlier, accompanied them on a hunting trip in South Texas. Barbara Bush had fallen in love with the charming canines, so the Vice President called and asked if there were any left in the litter. There was—a liver-colored female.

"Even on my most difficult and challenging days as President, Ranger and Millie brought great joy to my life. There is nothing like the unconditional love of a dog to help you get through the rough spots."

**Preceding Pages**
Beloved springer spaniel Millie lounges on a couch in the Red Room on the State Floor of the White House; one of many such images found in Millie's book.

**Right**
President Bush with Millie, at home in the private residence of the White House.

**Below**
Millie in the tulip garden of the Vice President's Residence.

It was the first female dog for the Bushes, and they named her Millie after a longtime family friend, Mildred Caldwell Kerr. The pup was a little more than a year old and originally destined to be a huntress, but due to her loving nature, Will Farish thought she would serve far better as a house dog. So off to training she went. As Mrs. Bush noted, "Training puppies on your own rugs is a challenge. Training pups on government rugs is impossible."

Millie was born January 12, 1985, and came to live with the Bushes on February 13, 1987, at the Vice President's Residence. Much like C. Fred, she became an instant member of the family, although, according to Millie herself, she had to work for it, as she recounted in her "memoir":

"It was love at first sight. Both Bushes kissed me, and I sat on Bar's lap all the way to Maine. I'm going to be honest (this is a confession that is difficult for me to make and you will understand why as you read on), Bar did whisper to me that night, 'You are so sweet, but you are so ugly. You have a pig's nose, you are bowlegged, and your eyes are yellow.' I knew immediately that I was going to have to try harder. She also told me that she really loved me. I believed her. That was sort of a rocky start, but I have since heard her tell others that she will never have another male dog again and that I am the best dog they ever lived with. I believe that too."

THE WHITE HOUSE
WASHINGTON

February 6, 1992

MEMO
IMPORTANT ANNOUNCEMENT

THIS IS AN ALL-POINTS BULLETIN FROM THE PRESIDENT

SUBJECT: MY DOG "RANGER"

Recently Ranger was put on a weight-reduction program. Either that program succeeds or we enter Ranger in the Houston Fat Stock Show as a Prime Hereford.

All offices should take a formal "pledge" that reads as follows: "WE AGREE NOT TO FEED RANGER. WE WILL NOT GIVE HIM BISCUITS. WE WILL NOT GIVE HIM FOOD OF ANY KIND."

In addition, Ranger's "access" is hereby restricted. He has been told not to wander the corridors without an escort. This applies to the East and West Wings, to the Residence from the 3rd floor to the very, very bottom basement.

Although Ranger will still be permitted to roam at Camp David, the Camp David staff including the Marines, Naval personnel, All Civilians and Kids are specifically instructed to "rat" on anyone seen feeding Ranger.

Ranger has been asked to wear a "Do not feed me" badge in addition to his ID.

I will, of course, report on Ranger's fight against obesity. Right now he looks like a blimp, a nice friendly appealing blimp, but a blimp.

We Need Your Help-All hands, please help.

FROM THE PRESIDENT

G. Bush

**Opposite**
First Lady Barbara Bush, Millie, and one of Millie's puppies venture out onto the South Lawn, April 13, 1989.

**Left**
Mrs. Bush and Millie watch President Bush play tennis at Walker's Point, Kennebunkport, Maine, August 7, 1991.

**Below**
As Marine One lands, President and Mrs. Bush are greeted by one of their grandchildren, Ellie LeBlond, along with Ranger and Millie.

The First Lady wasn't alone in remarking on Millie's looks. In July 1989, *Washingtonian* magazine named Millie "Ugliest Mutt," but many quickly came to her defense. Letters of support poured in. Canine organizations were outraged and sent press releases stating that an attack on First Dog Millie was an attack on all dogs.

Eventually the editors of the magazine apologized and sent Millie some dog biscuits. The President graciously accepted the apology and wrote to the editor, "Dear Jack: Not to worry! Millie, you see, likes publicity. She is hoping to parlay this into a Lassie-like Hollywood career. Seriously, no hurt feelings; but you are nice to write. Arf, arf for the dog biscuits. Sincerely, George Bush."

Millie commanded the spotlight even during the days when she held Second Dog rank (meaning she was the vice presidential pup). She posed for *Vanity Fur* and participated in various frivolities, such as a party with fellow Washington dogs. The Republican Pet Fete included Boxcar Willie Reagan, Maureen Reagan's dog; Blazer Luger; and Senator and Mrs. Bentley's Baby Bleep Bentley of Maryland.

In the fall of 1988, George Bush won the presidential election, and the family, Millie included, started packing for the People's House. Life in the White House was much different from life in the Vice President's Residence for President and Mrs. Bush—and for Millie. As Mrs. Bush recalled, "Another big change occurred when Millie came home to her new life. We were so glad to see her, but there was a big difference between opening the door at the Vice President's Residence (where there wasn't a soul around) in your bathrobe and letting the dog out at 6 a.m. and throwing on your warm-up suit at the White House (where the morning crew already was hard at work), waiting for the elevator to take you down two floors, racing down a long corridor through the diplomatic Reception Room, and

## THE GREAT BROWN-AND-WHITE HUNTER

As the transition of power from President Reagan to President Bush was about to take place, President Reagan heard of Millie's hunting activities at the Vice President's Residence on the U.S. Naval Observatory—particularly the decimation of the squirrel population—and was concerned on the squirrels' behalf. (He loved to feed them outside the Oval Office with nuts from Camp David.) So the day before he left the White House, he invited President-Elect Bush over to see a sign he had made. The custom "Beware of Dog" warning was placed alongside tree pots just outside the door to the Oval Office. Millie made good on the cautionary note, and by the spring of 1990, the count stood at "eight known kills—that is, done in full sight of people—four squirrels, three rats, and, to Bar's great sorrow, a pigeon."

**Left**
Millie sits next to the "Beware of Dog" sign left in the yard outside the Oval Office door by President Ronald Reagan, as a warning to the "pet" squirrels he was leaving behind.

**Right**
Millie lends a hand at the White House switchboard, July 7, 1989.

**Below**
Mrs. Bush, Ranger, and Millie wear matching gray sweat suits around the White House, January 9, 1991.

**Opposite Top**
Mrs. Bush and granddaughter Marshall peek at Millie and her newborn pups, March 18, 1989. The box, created by White House staff, bore the presidential seal.

**Opposite Bottom**
The First Lady takes Millie's puppies out for a walk in the White House Rose Garden, May 10, 1989.

out to the South Grounds. Gradually the butlers took over this job."

In an interview with *Life Magazine*, Mrs. Bush once recounted Millie's usual daily routine at the White House. "I walk her at 6 a.m. and feed her—kibble only. She gets White House table scraps when the President slips them to her. [President Bush] gives her showers—how else do you wash your dog? Every week or two we climb in the shower with our dog. We use dog shampoo. She has her own bed in our bedroom. She doesn't always choose it but she has one. ... Millie goes to the Oval Office every morning at 7 and has a little visit there, a little spoiling, plays a bit, and then comes home."

Not too long after her arrival at the White House, it was announced that First Dog Millie was pregnant. Earlier that year, during inaugural festivities for President Bush, Millie had been sent back to her old farm in Kentucky to meet her suitor, Tug Farish, who had been chosen by Will Farish to sire the pups. Once the happy news was made public, everyone began marking the days leading up to the delivery, and a Washington, D.C., paper even printed a

**Preceding Pages**
President Bush spends some quality time with Millie and her offspring on the South Lawn, April 20, 1989.

**Right**
The President takes time to enjoy Millie and her puppies, May 4, 1989.

**Below**
President and Mrs. Bush, along with Millie, deplane Air Force One.

**Opposite**
Mrs. Bush visits with Millie before a state dinner, June 27, 1989.

countdown as the nation eagerly awaited the puppies' arrival. And just as they had for the Fords, the carpenters of the White House, part of the Executive Residence staff, crafted a birthing box, complete with the presidential seal.

Millie gave birth to six pups—five females and one male—and the country fell in love immediately. First Lady Barbara Bush, Millie, and her pups posed for the covers of countless magazines, including *Life*. Tim McBride, special assistant to the President of the United States and personal aide, recalls how the arrival of Millie's puppies wreaked havoc on the President's daily schedule, which otherwise was planned to the minute. After the puppies were born, and during the weeks that followed, the President sought regular reports on their progress. Normally a punctual man, the President thought nothing of zipping over to the South Lawn or the residence to see firsthand what Millie and pups were up to. "But Mr. President," McBride would protest, "we don't have time. The foreign minister will be here any minute." But President Bush would not be persuaded. "This will only take a few minutes," he'd insist. He was the President, after all, and these were the First Puppies.

Several of Millie's offspring remained with the Bush family. Spot Fletcher (named for Texas Rangers baseball player Scott Fletcher) went to Texas to live with George W. Bush and his family. (She would eventually return to the White House when President George W. Bush was elected to office, making her the

only known pet to live at 1600 Pennsylvania Avenue under two administrations.) Camie went to live in Florida with Jeb Bush and his family. Ranger, the only male pup, was given to Marshall Bush, the daughter of Margaret and Marvin. The others went to friends.

The summer of 1990 was a rough one for Millie, who had been limping and crying. Eventually she was diagnosed with lupus. Vets closely monitored her condition and regulated it with medicine so that Millie would continue to feel fit. Once her illness became public, she received 382 get-well cards, then an additional 122 notes following an article in *Good Housekeeping*—a little glimpse of fan mail to come. Eventually the mail room of the White House assigned Millie her own volunteer, Jean Richards, to answer her correspondence. Millie also received presents and portraits.

During her term as First Lady, Barbara Bush released the No. 1 best-seller *Millie's Book: As Dictated to Barbara Bush.* It was written from Millie's point of view, recounting her life story plus many details about the White House, its history, and the lives of President and Mrs. Bush. The book was an instant hit. More than 400,000 copies were printed, eventually spawning editions in paperback and in German and Japanese. The book raised more than $1 million for the Barbara Bush Foundation for Literacy. Mr. Bush joked that although he was President of the United States, his dog made more money than he did.

In the fall of 1991, President Bush got his own dog—Ranger, the male from Millie's litter, with whom he had bonded when the dog was a puppy. Before Ranger was given to granddaughter Marshall Bush, who lived in D.C., President Bush often called to ask if Ranger wanted to accompany the family to Camp David for the weekend. When he began suggesting that Ranger arrive on Thursday to ensure he would be ready for the Friday departure and not return home until Tuesday, it was decided it would be better if Ranger moved to the White House permanently.

The Bushes, especially the President, adored having Ranger with them at Camp David. When he wasn't chasing deer or following Millie through the woods, Ranger was almost always at the President's side. Ranger loved the daily jogs with the President along the camp's perimeter. But at night, when President and Mrs. Bush turned out the lights at Aspen, their cabin, the exuberant puppy still wanted to play with Millie. Ranger made such a fuss that it was impossible for the First Couple to sleep. Before long, Mrs. Bush announced new cabin assignments; Ranger would be cabin mates with Tim McBride—at least at bedtime. Each night thereafter, McBride brought Ranger to his cabin, Redbud, where the dog slept peacefully

**Preceding Pages**
Larry King interviews Millie following the release of her book, October 4, 1992.

President Bush walks Millie and Ranger at Camp David, November 15, 1991.

Russian President Boris Yeltsin poses on the South Lawn of the White House with President and Mrs. Bush, Millie, and Ranger, June 16, 1992.

**Above**
Ranger and Millie enjoy the 18 acres that make up the White House grounds, May 25, 1992.

**Opposite**
The First Lady taking one of her many walks around the South Grounds of the White House with Millie, February 8, 1989.

on his bed. Ranger rejoined a well-rested President and Mrs. Bush the next morning.

Barbara Bush described Ranger as "a big, bouncy puppy; he could leap straight up into the air and his handsome face made us laugh. He charged around Camp David in the snow and the rain, and he wandered the White House, knowing no strangers. He loved to curl up by George's side and was everything in a dog George wanted. Ranger made so many friends that we suddenly noticed that he was growing by leaps and bounds—out, not up—and George had to send out a memo requesting people not feed Ranger."

Millie and Ranger were much loved by the Bushes, the White House staff, and the media. The hit TV show *Murphy Brown* had an episode about Millie. Judith Leiber, the longtime celebrated purse designer, even made a jeweled handbag designed after her. Roland Mesnier, executive White House pastry chef for more than six presidents, described Millie as "presidential to the core." When Mrs. Bush sat down, so would Millie. When Mrs. Bush got up, Millie would follow. And, Mesnier claims, she never barked!

In the opening to her autobiography, *A Memoir*, Barbara Bush described their last few hours at the White House before the historical transfer of power to the Clinton Administration. They spent part of those last precious moments with their dogs.

"We started the day as we did every morning, waking up about 5:30 a.m., ringing the bell for the butlers, and drinking coffee in bed while reading the papers. Our phone started ringing immediately with our children checking in to make sure we were okay. Later in the morning, George called me from the Oval Office and asked if I wanted to walk around the South Grounds with the dogs just one more time. It was a glorious, sunny day. The dogs ran and chased squirrels and dashed around looking for who knows what. The pleasure George got from his dog Ranger taking flying leaps over imaginary logs cannot be described. … We have always lived in happy houses, but nothing matched this special place."

Today a dog park in Houston is named for Millie. President and Mrs. Bush continue to uphold their reputation as dog lovers and currently own a pair of Maltipoos, BiBi and Mini Me.

# The *Clinton* Years

**1993–2001**

**SOCKS ★ BUDDY**

**President William Jefferson Clinton**, his wife, Hillary Rodham Clinton, and their daughter, Chelsea, entered the White House on January 20, 1993, with a little black-and-white cat named Socks. Socks and Buddy the dog, who President Clinton acquired in his second term, became mascots for the Clinton White House and soared to levels of popularity never seen before, in part due to the emergence of the internet. The First Lady further secured their place in history with her book *Dear Socks, Dear Buddy: Kids' Letters to the First Pets.*

Socks moved into the Executive Mansion with the Clintons after a two-day car trip from Little Rock, Arkansas. The family had adopted him in March 1991, while Clinton was still governor of Arkansas. The story goes that the furry feline jumped into the arms—and heart—of daughter Chelsea as she was leaving the home of her piano teacher. Socks was a domestic shorthair with yellow-green eyes. He weighed nine pounds and was roughly a foot tall with black-and-white markings.

The First Cat had to adjust to life as First Pet. During his days at the Governor's Mansion in Arkansas, he was allowed to roam freely and was known as a great explorer. However, the White House, on 18 acres and surrounded by an iron fence he could easily fit through, was feared to be too large and daunting a territory for a lone feline. So Socks was allowed to prowl the South Lawn only on a very long leash. One of his favorite spots was behind the Oval Office, where Betty Currie, the President's secretary, could kept her eye on him. He was also quite fond of the pin oak planted by President Dwight D. Eisenhower and his wife, Mamie. Inside the White House his location of choice was a wing chair in the receiving room outside the Oval Office. He was also mesmerized by the visitor's office, which was home to a three-story cat house, complete with a scratching post—a gift from an admirer in Florida. For several months during his tenure, Socks befriended a stray tabby nicknamed Slippers and without reservation shared his food and water with the other cat.

Socks was the principal First Pet during Clinton's first term. As such, he was the character the Clinton White House employed to welcome children to its website. A cartoon version of the cat was created to guide kids through the site and invite them to learn White House history and seek out other fun activities. Socks' stats page stated that he loved to catch spiders and take catnaps. Being only the fourth cat to live at 1600 Pennsylvania Avenue since the days of Franklin D. Roosevelt in 1933, he became something of a celebrity for cat lovers around the world and was celebrated in poems, commemorated on a postage stamp by the Central African Republic, and regarded as a well-known figure by the media.

It was not until President Clinton's second term, after Chelsea had left for college, that President and Mrs. Clinton decided to get another pet—a dog.

**Preceding Pages**
Inauguration Day, January 20, 1993: President and Mrs. Bush greet President-Elect and Mrs. Clinton and daughter Chelsea upon the family's arrival at the White House, prior to the drive to the Capitol. The Bushes' dog, Ranger, participates in the amiable transfer of power.

Socks commands the podium in the White House briefing room.

**Right**
President and Mrs. Clinton on the White House lawn with Socks, February 24, 1997.

**Below**
President Clinton as a child in Hot Springs, Arkansas, with his older half-brother, Roger, and his childhood pet, King, a German shepherd.

Both had grown up with animals, including dogs. The President had a beloved German shepherd named King who was commemorated by White House Pastry Chef Roland Mesnier. The chef designed a Christmas gingerbread house replicating the President's childhood home in Hope, Arkansas, complete with a marzipan version of King sitting on the front porch. And the Clintons' first pet together was a butterscotch-colored cocker spaniel named Zeke. He was a gift from Mrs. Clinton to the President before Chelsea was born, and he lived with the Clintons for several years. The entire family was saddened when he died after being hit by a car. It was not until December 1997 that the Clintons once again had a dog in their family.

The President was immediately taken with the Labrador retriever they called Buddy. (Alas, the same could not be said of Socks.) Born on August 7, 1997,

**Left**
Socks marvels at his many likenesses in Executive Pastry Chef Roland Mesnier's traditional gingerbread house. The chef was particularly fond of this creation, which became known as the House of Socks, as it contained 21 miniature marzipan versions of the First Feline.

**Below**
For the 1998 gingerbread house, Mesnier created whimsical cookie replicas of First Pets Buddy and Socks dancing together.

Buddy's color was pure chocolate, and his eyes were hazel. Mrs. Clinton recalled that one of the first challenges was picking the perfect name. Hundreds of suggestions poured into the White House. Some of her favorites included Barkansas, Arkanpaws, and Clin Tin Tin. Another suggestion was Top Secret. President and Mrs. Clinton narrowed the list to seven names and then waited for Chelsea to come home for a visit from college to select the final one. And Buddy it was, after one of the President's favorite uncles, Oren Grisham, whose nickname was just that. The uncle, who had passed away by the time the pup arrived, raised and trained dogs for more than 50 years, and the President had fond memories of visiting him and playing with the dogs.

Like Socks, Buddy had his preferred places in the White House. Following breakfast and his daily walk, he usually accompanied the President to the Oval Office, where the sunny window was one of his favorite spots to catch a snooze. Buddy did, of course, have his share of scene-stealing moments in the Oval Office. One time he jumped up in a chair next to Secretary Madeleine Albright during a most formal foreign policy meeting. He

was closest to President Clinton, and one of his famous tricks included standing on his hind legs, putting his paws on the President's chest, and giving him "kisses and hugs." And following in the footsteps of the Nixon and Ford retrievers, Buddy relished a swim in the famous fountain that he and his canine predecessors viewed as their personal swimming hole.

Buddy almost put his mark—quite literally—on the Christmas décor in 1998, when one of the edible creations was nearly destroyed. The President, Mrs. Clinton, and Chelsea, were making their annual surprise visit to the Grand Foyer to thank all the volunteers who were hurriedly putting the final touches on the decorations. That year they strolled in accompanied by Prime Minister Jean Chretien of Canada, who happened to be in town, and Buddy. The volunteers were so excited that no one noticed Buddy making a beeline for a tantalizing confection on a pier table. The President caught him just in the nick of time. After that, reporters were told, Buddy was put under 24-hour guard for the duration of the holiday season.

In 1998, Mrs. Clinton published the best-selling book *Dear Socks, Dear Buddy: Kids' Letters to the First Pets*. The 255-page book included fun anecdotes from both Buddy and Socks of their days at the White House and accounts of activities they enjoyed, such as visiting hospitals and greeting guests at the Executive Mansion. What made the book so unique, however, were more than 50 letters from children across the country to the First Pets, including exacting notes of good wishes ("I want to give you a big heart, as big as the whole world") to generous words of wisdom ("Just because they went on a trip and didn't take you doesn't mean they don't love you anymore").

**Preceding Pages**
President Clinton tosses a ball for Buddy on the South Lawn.

**Opposite**
The First Lady relaxes with Socks and Buddy in April 1999.

**Above**
A greeting card featuring Socks was sent to many of the First Cat's admirers.

**Opposite**
Buddy brings a ball to President Clinton.

**Left**
Socks poses on the South Lawn during the annual White House Easter Egg Roll.

**Below**
A candid close-up of First Dog Buddy.

The First Lady wrote in the foreword of the book: "Over the years, Socks has heard from animal lovers of all ages, including admirers from England, Bangladesh, and nearly 50 other countries, who have written asking for celebrity shots and 'paw-tographs' (his paw print signature). And since our chocolate Labrador retriever, Buddy, bounded into our lives, he has acquired lots of pen pals of his own. Together, Socks and Buddy have received more than 300,000 letters and e-mails, as well as hundreds of handcrafted gifts. ... Assembling these letters from children to Socks and Buddy gives me the opportunity to share with you some of the many laughs and loving moments that Bill, Chelsea, and I have enjoyed with our pets." Proceeds from the book benefited the National Park Foundation.

The Clinton White House Staff did its best to answer most all the letters they received, especially those from children to the pets. The retired service personnel who live at the U.S. Soldiers' and Airmens' Home in Washington, D.C., helped deal with the mail and reply to it; sometimes Socks would visit

## FAMILY FEUD

One of Washington's favorite White House episodes was the now-famed meeting between Socks and Buddy. Needless to say, Socks was less than thrilled about Buddy's arrival and, in fact, found his intrusion intolerable. President Clinton said, "I did better with...the Palestinians and the Israelis than I've done with Socks and Buddy." Following an encounter that resulted in a good swat to Buddy from Socks, the two seemed to reach somewhat of a compromise and did their best to get along.

**Left**
Buddy and Socks convene outside the Oval Office.

BUDD

"It wasn't until Socks arrived with his toy mouse and Buddy walked in with his rawhide bone that this house became a home. Pets have a way of doing that."

Hillary Rodham Clinton

**Preceding Pages**
President Clinton on the South Lawn of the White House with Buddy.

**Right**
Buddy demands some attention from the President in the Oval Office.

**Right**
The First Family—Buddy included—leaves the White House for a vacation.

**Opposite**
President Clinton with Buddy in the ground floor corridor of the White House.

them to express his appreciation. Most would receive a photo of one of the First Pets complete with paw print and message.

Buddy and Socks were hugely popular during their days at the White House, and Buddy the dog was the most widely photographed pet that had ever lived at the White House. When the Clintons left the White House in 2001, they took Buddy to their new home in New York, and Socks went to live with Betty Currie. Buddy, sadly, was struck by a car while the President and Mrs. Clinton were out of town and died in 2002. Socks lived approximately 20 years and passed on February 20, 2009, in Hollywood, Maryland, after suffering from cancer of the jaw. The pets retained their popularity in their post-White House years, and newspapers reported their deaths with heavy hearts.

In her book, Mrs. Clinton wrote about the transition to the White House and the wonderful sentiment animals can bring: "When we moved to Washington from Little Rock, we brought our family traditions, favorite pictures, and personal mementos to make the White House feel more comfortable. But it wasn't until Socks arrived with his toy mouse and Buddy walked in with his rawhide bone that this house became a home. Pets have a way of doing that."

# The Bush Years

## 2001–2009

SPOT ★ BARNEY ★ MISS BEAZLEY ★ INDIA "KITTY"

**President George W. Bush** took the oath of office in 2001. He had a deep appreciation and love for animals, sentiments he and First Lady Laura Bush—and their daughters—brought with them from Texas to the White House. They moved into 1600 Pennsylvania with two dogs and a cat. One of the dogs, Spot, holds a special place in presidential history as the only dog to have lived in the White House under two different administrations. During their eight years in America's home, the Bushes lost two cherished pets, but they also welcomed a new one. They also maintained a "Western White House" at their ranch in Crawford, Texas, where a larger menagerie of animals was kept, including some Texas longhorns.

George W. was indulged with many pet dogs during his childhood in Texas; not surprisingly, because his parents, President George H.W. and Barbara Bush, were also dog lovers. They had a collie named Mark and a poodle mix called Nicky, just to name a few. This fondness for animals was something that the Bushes wanted to instill in their twin daughters, Jenna and Barbara.

Laura Bush also had many pets growing up, including Bully the terrier; Rusty the cocker spaniel; Roman, a Dalmatian mix; Duke the boxer; Freckles, a springer mix; a beagle mix named Bo; Marty the mutt; and Tom the cat. She also had a box turtle that lived on the back porch and horny toads in the garden. "We laughed over the antics of our animals, and they were our beloved companions," recalled the First Lady in her autobiography. "We were warmed by their unconditional love. I played with the dogs and dressed my cat in doll clothes. Time and time again, our animals found us, arriving as if by canine or feline navigation at our front door." Before she got married, Laura had a cat she called Dewey, for the Dewey Decimal System. She got Dewey when she moved to Austin, and he moved back with her to Midland.

Mrs. Bush fondly remembers the naming of their pets with her husband and the girls: "All our animals in Dallas were named for Texas Rangers baseball players. Spot got her name in honor of infielder Scott Fletcher, Barbara's favorite player. Of course, the Rangers traded Scott almost immediately. Our cat was named after Ruben Sierra, whose nickname, El Indio, gave Kitty her name, India. At times, I would look at our pets and remember our girls and our lives, the family that we were beyond the White House walls."

Spot was the daughter of the famous Millie, First Pet of President and Mrs. George H.W. Bush, and she was born at the White House before moving to Dallas to live with Laura and George Bush. Because she had been at the White house before, she had a history with the staff too. "It was so exciting for many of the residence staff to see Spot back at the White House again," recalled Roland Mesnier, executive White House pastry chef for more than 25 years and

UNITED STATES OF AMERICA

five administrations. "Personally, I was so glad to see my friend again."

Shortly after the historic 2001 election, Christine Todd Whitman, President Bush's choice for the administrator of the Environmental Protection Agency, gave the new President and First Lady a Scottish terrier they named Barney. Whitman was the owner of Coors, Barney's mother. Barney became a mascot of sorts for the White House and an instant member of the family. Soon he evolved into a star attraction.

Mrs. Bush remembers first meeting Barney: "I finished that day by interviewing potential staff members for my new East Wing office at the White House. The last candidate had four legs and was 10 weeks old. He was a Scottish terrier puppy, born to a dog owned by New Jersey Governor Christine Todd Whitman, and, of course, I fell in love. I had seen his pictures on November 4, my birthday, when George and I were in New Jersey on the last leg of the campaign trail. George hadn't gotten me a gift, and Christine suggested a puppy. Our D.C. interview sealed the deal. Barney flew back with me to Austin the next day to join our animal family."

The Bushes' pets were true ambassadors, often appearing on Christmas cards, as Christmas tour guides, as part of the Easter Egg Roll, and more. Mrs. Bush not only showered her pets with love and affection, but she also celebrated all animals in her 2002 Christmas theme, 'All Creatures Great and Small". During that holiday, papier-mâché replicas of prior First Pets were displayed throughout the White House.

The savvy First Lady also used the family's pets as a way to open the doors of the First Residence to more people than ever before, thereby making their animals some of the best known in presidential history. On August 31, 2001, just months after entering

**Preceding Page**
President George W. Bush and First Pet Spot walk across the South Lawn following the President's arrival aboard Marine One, January 15, 2002.

**Opposite**
Republican presidential candidate Texas Gov. George W. Bush and running mate Dick Cheney walk down a dirt road to meet with reporters, followed by Bush's dog Spot, in Crawford, Texas, November 11, 2000.

**Above**
Spot stands patiently next to Marine honor guards as he waits for the rest of the First Family to join him in departing Camp David aboard Marine One for their return to Washington, D.C., December 26, 2001.

**Opposite**
President George W. Bush spends a quiet moment with First Dogs Barney and Spot in the Stateroom aboard Air Force One, en route to Waco from Dobbins Air Force Base in Marietta, Georgia, February 20, 2003.

**Left**
President Bush takes a moment to see First Dog Spot on the South Lawn of the White House.

**Below**
Mrs. Bush offers photos of the Bush family dogs, Scottish terriers Barney and Miss Beazley, and the cat, India, to a little girl before departing from Forbes Field in Topeka, Kansas, September 16, 2008. She had just greeted members of the military gathered to see her departure from the airfield.

the executive mansion, the President and First Lady unveiled a new White House website (designed especially for their administration), with links to presidential announcements, briefings, appointments, and radio addresses, as well as a highly interactive children's segment, where kids were welcomed online by presidential pooches Spot and Barney. India the cat and Ofelia the longhorn had a web presence as well, and the kids' link incorporated a photo album and virtual tour of the White House, with lessons on American heroes, history quizzes, and holiday coloring pages, among other fun activities. Whitehousekids.gov was an instant success and eventually included bio pages for all the First Pets, including Barney, Spot, India, Ofelia, and Jackson and Dave—Vice President Dick Cheney's dogs. The site became so popular that Barney got his own web address: barney.gov.

At a press conference, the President spoke jokingly of his dog's cyber status: "I was particularly impressed that Barney plays a major role in helping the young understand what's going on in Washington, D.C. I say that somewhat in jest, but I'm very serious about the need for all of us involved in government to do all we can to involve our citizenry in government. There is a lot of cynicism about politics in Washington, D.C.,

**Right**
Mrs. Bush and First Dog Barney look at Executive White House Pastry Chef Roland Mesnier's creation, a 40-pound semi-sweet chocolate Easter egg decorated with the First Family's dog, Barney, who is painting an Easter egg depicting Spot in the State Dining Room, April 1, 2002.

**Above**
President George W. Bush greets Israeli Prime Minister Ariel Sharon upon the prime minister's arrival to the President's ranch in Crawford, Texas, April 11, 2005.

**Opposite**
First Dog Barney steals the show in the Oval Office, May 18, 2004.

and it seems to me the more accessible Washington becomes, the more likely it is people will participate in the process."

Barney's celebrity status continued to grow. Following the September 11 tragedy, the White House was locked down, curtailing its usual traffic of tours. When the holidays approached, many people were disappointed they couldn't come inside and see the décor. But Barney saved the day. Wearing a tiny video camera on his collar, he scurried around the State Floor, taping a "tour" of the mansion's decorations. The end result was a four-and-a-half-minute video available for viewing on the White House website. Conceived as a way to share the decorations at the People's House with the people, the Barney Cam video was a hit, boasting 24 million viewings the day it was launched.

Due to its popularity, the Barney Cam became an annual holiday feature for the remainder of the Bush Administration. Occasionally a few other surprise films, such as My Barney Valentine, were introduced—with Barney in the starring role, of course. The clips developed more defined plotlines and even introduced celebrities in cameo roles, such as British Prime Minister Tony Blair, Karl Rove, and 2008 Olympic gold medalists Michael Phelps and Nastia Liukin.

The other animals got into the act as well—however briefly—as Mrs. Bush recalled. "One of our press aides, Jeanie Mamo, became an expert at launching

# FLYING FEATHERS

In 2006, Barney and Beazley had a close encounter of a turkey kind, during the pardoning event, an annual White House tradition since 1989 (when President George H.W. Bush officially pardoned a Thanksgiving turkey). On this day, President George W. Bush was having his weekly update with the FBI director. Both his secretary and personal aide were out, so David Sherzer, special projects coordinator in the Oval Office, was the only staff member manning the front office. Also out that day were White House Grounds Superintendent Dale Haney, the unofficial dog handler, and Sam Sutton, one of the President's valets who acted as backup handler.

Barney and Beazley were hanging out in the Rose Garden outside the Oval Office, minding their own business, while the Park Service guys set up chairs for the event. But when the people from the National Turkey Federation arrived, the dogs started barking.

"The President yelled out to me to get Dale to the dogs," Sherzer recalls. "I explained to him that both Dale and Sam were out, but I would get Robert, one of his other valets. Robert was on the third floor of the residence–probably a five-minute walk, so it took him a while to come down. Meanwhile, even though the dogs were going crazy, the people from the National Turkey Federation let the turkey, Flyer, out of its cage. The dogs went ballistic, chasing Flyer from one end of the Rose Garden to the other. Feathers were flying everywhere."

"The President burst out of his FBI briefing and shouted at me, 'Where is Robert?!?!' Then, as the Park Service and National Turkey Federation people watched stunned, the President chased down Barney and Beazley. It would have been a complete disaster if the dogs had eaten the turkey before it could be pardoned—so President Bush saved the turkey's life twice that day."

**Right**
First Dog Barney excitedly watches Flyer, the turkey selected to be pardoned at the National Thanksgiving Turkey Ceremony, November 22, 2006.

**Right**
First Pet Barney holds a press briefing, September 8, 2004.

**Below**
Laura Bush holds Miss Beazley shortly after the 10-week-old Scottish terrier's arrival to the White House, January 6, 2005.

bright plastic Christmas balls around the East Room, which Barney chased, slipping and sliding across the glossy waxed floors. ... One Barney Cam video ended with Kitty serenely sitting on my lap. Unlike our canines, she steadfastly refused to mug for the camera."

The First Lady outlined the First Pets' routines in one of her speeches: "Our dogs, Barney and Spot, and our cat, India, also feel very much at home in the White House. In fact, they are the only residents who make no distinction between the West and East Wings. Every morning, the President walks the dogs on his way to work. The dogs spend time playing in the garden, and then Spot retires to the Oval Office for her morning nap. Later, she joins Barney for an adventure along a well-worn path from the West Wing to the East Wing. [The] first stop is the medical unit for treats. Then to the Social Office in the East Wing, which has the best treats of all—and, finally, next door to the Military Office, where Barney barks like mad at the electric shoe polisher. Spot and Barney particularly enjoy their trek during the holidays. They not only get treats, but toys as well."

In addition to their packed city schedule, the pets accompanied the President and First Lady to all of the

**Left**
President George W. Bush and Barney at their favorite fishing spot at the Bush Ranch in Crawford, Texas, April 28, 2002.

**Opposite**
President George W. Bush walking down the steps of Air Force One with First Dogs Miss Beazley and Barney.

**Left**
Barbara Bush and Jenna Bush join Miss Beazley and Barney during a visit to the Lincoln Bedroom for the taping of Barney Cam, November 25, 2007.

**Below**
President George W. Bush spends a quiet morning moment with Spot and Barney in the Oval Office, September 17, 2002.

**Right**
White House pets India, Miss Beazley, and Barney get ready for Halloween on the South Lawn, October 31, 2007. India, as a wizard; Miss Beazley, as a strawberry; and Barney, as a cowboy.

**Below**
First Pets Barney, Miss Beazley, and India, the cat, pose for the cover of a cookbook presented to Mrs. Bush on her birthday by her staff.

**Left**
Barney watches as Miss Beazley gives a "kiss" to India the cat, as the White House pets pose for a Valentine's Day portrait in the Red Room of the White House, February 8, 2007.

**Below Left**
Barney celebrates his fourth birthday in the Palm Room of the White House, September 30, 2004.

**Below Right**
Vice President Dick Cheney's Labrador retrievers Jackson, dressed as Darth Vader, and Dave, dressed as Superman, prepare for Halloween at the Vice President's Residence at the Naval Observatory in Washington, D.C., October 30, 2007.

SONY
11-16-05

appropriate places, such as Camp David, even when visiting heads of state—such as British Prime Minister Tony Blair and his wife, Cherie—were present. On one visit, Laura Bush recalled worrying about the Blairs mingling with the animals: "The only thing I felt bad about on this visit was that I don't think the Blairs, Cherie especially, were all that keen on pets. We, of course, had ferried Kitty, Barney, and Spot to Camp David. I asked Cherie if they had any animals, and she paused and answered, 'Well, we had a gerbil. Once.'"

The First Pets weren't the only animals welcome at Camp David. Vice President Dick Cheney and his family spent many days at Camp David during his tenure, and Cheney distinctly recalls one episode with his Labrador Dave, who caused a bit of a ruckus.

"From the beginning, we brought our dog Dave, a hundred-pound yellow Lab, to Camp David. He loved roaming the paths and the woods, and I quickly got used to taking him everywhere with me. One weekend when the President had scheduled a National Security Council meeting at Camp David, I drove with Dave in one of the golf carts over to Laurel for breakfast. I parked the golf cart, and Dave and I walked down the path toward the big wooden doors of Laurel. I had briefing materials for the day's meetings and the morning newspaper under one arm and opened the door with the other. No sooner had we walked inside than Dave caught sight of the president's dog, Barney, and set off in hot pursuit.

"I couldn't really blame him. Barney was only slightly larger than the squirrels Dave loved chasing, but we didn't want any permanent harm to happen here. I dropped my papers so I could get hold of Dave, who by now had rounded the corner into the dining room. I rounded the same corner to encounter some of the cabinet spouses who had also been invited to Camp David for the weekend. Joyce Rumsfeld, Alma Powell, and

**Opposite**
Barney and Miss Beazley on the South Lawn of the White House filming the Barney Cam IV: "A Very Beazley Christmas," Christmas 2005.

**Above**
While filming the very first Barney Cam for Mrs. Bush's holiday theme, All Creatures Great and Small, the camera captures Barney's every move. He follows Spot as they take a look at the bird ornaments on the White House Christmas Tree in the Blue Room, December 9, 2002.

**Left**
Vice President Dick Cheney and Mrs. Cheney with their lab, Dave, on the porch of the Vice President's Residence on a beautiful Easter Sunday.

**Above**
Vice President Dick Cheney is joined by his dogs, Dave (left) and Jackson, during an interview with John King of CNN, at the Vice President's Residence at the Naval Observatory in Washington D.C., June 22, 2006.

**Right**
Anita McBride (left) and Andi Ball (right), incoming and outgoing chiefs of staff to First Lady Laura Bush, respectively, meet the Bushes' newest pet, Miss Beazley.

**Opposite**
Barney and Miss Beazley follow President Bush along the West Wing Colonnade, on their way back to the Oval Office, July 23, 2008.

Stephanie Tenet, all seated for breakfast, were watching aghast as Dave bounded around the dining table after a furiously scurrying Barney. At about that moment the President appeared. 'What's going on here?' he demanded. It was not an unreasonable question. I saw a tray of pastries on the breakfast buffet, grabbed one, and hollered, 'Dave, treat!' He stopped in his tracks, then I grabbed him and took him back to Dogwood, the cabin in which Lynne and I were staying. I hadn't been there long when there was a knock at the door. It was the camp commander. 'Mr. Vice President,' he said, 'your dog has been banned from Laurel.'"

It turns out that the Bushes also found a fellow dog lover in Russian President Vladimir Putin, with whom President Bush also shared a little friendly competition. "Putin and I both loved physical fitness," recalled President Bush. "Vladimir worked out hard, swam regularly, and practiced judo. We were both competitive people. On his visit to Camp David, I introduced him to our Scottish terrier, Barney. He wasn't very impressed. On my next trip to Russia, Vladimir asked if I wanted to meet his dog, Koni. 'Sure,' I said. As we walked the birch-lined grounds of his dacha, a big, black labrador came charging across the lawn. With a twinkle in his eye, Vladimir said, 'Bigger, stronger, and faster than Barney.' I later told the story to my friend, Prime Minister Stephan Harper of Canada. 'You're lucky he only showed you his dog,' he replied."

In 2004, a bittersweet moment came to the White House with the passing of Spot. After 15 years as a member of the family, she suffered a stroke. Members of the White House staff were notified that Spot would have to be put down and were given time if they wanted to say good-bye to her. Because many of them had known her under both administrations, they were grateful for the chance. Laura Bush remembered the sad moment.

"Spot, our beloved springer spaniel, died that winter. I was away when she suffered a stroke. The only humane thing to do was put her to sleep, but George waited for me to return, so that I too would have a chance to say good-bye. The evening before Spot was going to be put down, George lovingly carried her out to the South Lawn, on whose lush grass she had rolled as a puppy and where, even as an old girl, she loved to chase after balls. George laid her down and then got down on the grass himself, encircling her in the chill dusk with the warmth of his body and gently stroking her head for a final farewell."

"Our pets have been such a source of comfort and entertainment to us. We've laughed over the antics of our animals, and we've been warmed by their unconditional love."

Laura Bush

**Preceding Pages**
On an overcast afternoon, Barney and Miss Beazley relax on the South Lawn, with the Jefferson Memorial in the background, March 26, 2007.

**Right**
President and Mrs. Bush walking First Dogs Barney and Spot to Air Force One departing Texas in June 2001.

In 2005, for Mrs. Bush's birthday, the President presented her with Miss Beazley, another Scottish terrier. The 10-week-old puppy arrived on January 6. In true White House fashion, Miss Beazley started her first day at the White House with a press conference introducing her to the world.

Anita McBride, Mrs. Bush's chief of staff, vividly remembers Miss Beazley's arrival: "It was eagerly anticipated by Mrs. Bush. It was on the official schedule for the day. I had only been on the job for a few weeks, but I quickly learned how the 'power of the pets' impacted daily life in the White House. I was somewhat prepared for it because of my husband's experience as personal aide to former president George H.W. Bush when Millie's puppies were born in 1989. Visiting the pups at any time of the day was important to Bush 41. The same was true whenever there was a sighting of Miss Beazley and Barney moving freely about the White House. They loved the East Wing, and our staff loved having them around too. But we were under strict instructions from the President: 'Do not feed the dogs.'"

Miss Beazley was a welcome addition to the First Family and became a great playmate for Barney. She was included in the famous Barney Cam videos, and she was given a bio page of her own on the website. Baseball cards featuring the Bushes' White House pets were favorites of children, who relished the portrait and bio on the front and back. There were even signed—or pawed, rather—photographs of the First Pets, along with stickers that read, "Miss Beazley believes in you."

One of Anita McBride's favorite memories happened in 2008. "Every year, Mrs. Bush's staff would think of fun and creative gifts to give her for her birthday in November and for Christmas. As the administration was drawing to a close, we would often hear Mrs. Bush say how after 14 years of having a chef, in the Texas Governor's Mansion and the White House, she didn't know if she could even cook anymore. We thought it would be a fun idea to collect all of our favorite family recipes and put them together in a cookbook for her.

"For the cover we staged Barney, Beazley, and Kitty sitting at the small table in the family kitchen wearing chef's hats and neckerchiefs and perusing the new cookbook. Mrs. Bush's aide, Lindsey Knutson, and White House Chef Cris Cumerford staged the photo-op for White House photographer Joyce Naltchayan. The pets were perfect actors, although we did have to Photoshop India. We all got a good laugh—including the President—over our creative, and useful, gift for Mrs. Bush's final birthday in the White House."

In the epilogue of his autobiography, *Decision Points*, President Bush made lighthearted mention of life after the White House for both himself and Barney: "Every now and then, there are reminders of how much life has changed. Shortly after we moved to Dallas, I took Barney for an early morning walk around the neighborhood. I hadn't done anything like that in more than a decade. Barney never had—he'd spent his entire life at the White House, Camp David, and Crawford. Barney spotted our neighbor's lawn, where he promptly took care of his business. There I was, the former President of the United States, with a plastic bag on my hand, picking up that which I had been dodging for the past eight years."

After serving many First Families, Roland Mesnier says that he thinks the Bushes are perhaps the biggest pet lovers to have called 1600 Pennsylvania Avenue home. He says that not only did the Bush family treat their animals with respect, but they also loved their pets as members of the family. Sadly, their cat India passed away shortly before the Bushes' left the White House.

The public and the press loved the Bushes' four-legged friends, too. "Mrs. Bush used to say that pets help make a house a home, and there was no bigger treat for a White House tourist than to catch a glimpse of Barney or Beazley," recalls White House Press Secretary Dana Perino. "The press loved any news or stories about the pets. You never got bad coverage when the dogs were involved."

# The *Obama* Years

## 2009–PRESENT

★BO★

**President Barack Obama** took office in January 2009. The former senator from Illinois and his family came to the White House without a pet. But what the new President and First Lady did bring with them was significant: the promise of a dog for their two young daughters, Sasha and Malia. The nation watched and waited—and offered opinions, of course—in anticipation of the addition to America's First Family.

On November 4, 2008, President-Elect Obama gave his widely televised victory speech in Chicago's Grant Park. One statement that received a lot of attention—and warranted many TV replays—was his vow to make good on his word to his young daughters. "Sasha and Malia, I love you both so much ... and you have earned the new puppy that's coming with us to the White House!"

The country went wild with speculation. Blogs, magazines, and newspapers were filled with conjecture and suggestions about what type of dog the President and First Lady should select for their girls. At his first press conference, reporters hounded President Obama with breed-specific questions. He replied, "Our preference would be to get a shelter dog, but, obviously, a lot of shelter dogs are mutts like me." He also noted that "Malia is allergic, so it has to be hypoallergenic. There are a number of breeds that are hypoallergenic." And so the hunt for the perfect pet was on.

Offers poured in from dog lovers wanting to give America's new First Family a canine from every breed imaginable. Even Claudia Galvez, head of the Friends of the Peruvian Hairless Dog Association, offered Little Machu Picchu—a Peruvian hairless dog—with hopes of eluding Malia's allergies. Just days before the historic inauguration, in an interview with George Stephanopoulos, the President-Elect stated that the family had narrowed down the choices to a Labradoodle or a Portuguese water dog. "We're closing in on it," he shared. "This has been tougher than finding a commerce secretary."

Although people across the country lobbied for a variety of dogs—someone even launched a blog called Labradoodle for Obama—in the end, the Portuguese water dog prevailed. The breed is known for its high spirits and for being a good fit for kids with allergies. The dog was a gift from Senator Ted Kennedy, who owned three of the same breed. One of his pups, Cappy (Amigo's Captain Courageous), and the Obamas' dog (named Bo by the girls), are two of nine siblings from a litter in Texas. The litter itself was named Hope and Change, in honor of the Obama victory.

On April 12, 2009, a formal announcement was made that the First Family would soon welcome the 6-month-old puppy into the White House. The dog visited the family some weeks earlier in a secret meeting to gauge compatibility; however, the gift was not official until April 14, 2009, when the dog moved in. At that point, a photo op took place, capturing the Obama family and Bo on the South Lawn. At the accompanying news conference, the President was asked if he would allow Bo inside the Oval Office, to which he responded, "Of course."

**Preceding Page**
Bo chases President Barack Obama on the South Lawn of the White House, May 12, 2009.

**Right**
First dog Bo climbs the stairs of Air Force One at Andrews Air Force Base, Maryland, for a flight to Chicago with President Barack Obama, August 4, 2010.

SIDENT OF THE
E PLURIBUS UNUM
ATES

**Opposite**
The Obama family welcomes Bo, the new family pet, to the White House.

**Left**
White House pastry chefs decorate cookies shaped like Bo for holiday receptions at the White House, December 8, 2010.

**Below**
Bo, sporting a Hawaiian lei, arrives at the White House.

Bo arrived wearing a colorful lei, in honor of the President's Hawaiian roots. Although the dog is registered with the American Kennel Club as Amigo's New Hope, the Obama girls call him Bo, after their cousin's cats, Bo and Diddley, and for the First Lady's father, who is nicknamed Diddley. So Bo is actually a namesake of R&B legend Bo Diddley.

In his first few months at the White House, Bo attended training to learn how to sit, heel, and shake a paw on command. However, the First Lady admitted during an interview, he wasn't without his flaws. He was caught tearing up magazines and going after the President's gym shoes. But what puppy hasn't done that?

President Obama told one television interviewer that his nighttime walks with the new family pet were the highlight of his days. "I'm the guy with the night shift. We go out and we're walking and in the background is the beautifully lit White House. It's quite a moment."

In June 2009, the White House released a baseball card with Bo's official portrait on one side and tongue-in-cheek statistics on the other. His favorite food? Tomatoes. Running is his favorite exercise, and he loves to nap near the Obama girls. His favorite hobbies are

"Bo is the most famous member
of the Obama family."

Michelle Obama

**Preceding Pages**
Bo, the Obama family pet, plays in the snow during a blizzard on the south grounds of the White House, February 10, 2010.

**Left**
President Obama plays with Bo aboard Air Force One during a flight to Hawaii, December 23, 2011.

playing on the White House lawn and going on walks with the family. And his goal as First Dog? To make friends with foreign dognitaries. The card is available by sending a self-addressed stamped envelope to the White House.

Not surprisingly, Bo became a media darling right away, and both the President and Mrs. Obama have joked that he is the most popular member of the White House. Bo appeared on Oprah's Christmas special in 2009 sporting a Christmas collar bedecked with little bells. He stole the show when he showed off his trick: giving a high-five to the First Lady and Oprah. During that interview, the First Lady commented, "Bo does not need a buddy," effectively letting the country know that he would remain the only First Dog for the time being.

For his first summer vacation, Bo accompanied the family on Air Force One to Martha's Vineyard, and he has been included on most family trips since. Perhaps most sensational was his trip to Hawaii for Christmas 2010. A Politico.com headline claimed "Bo Gets Quarantined," but that was a bit of an overstatement. In reality, even the First Family had to follow the rules

**Opposite Top**
Bo paws First Lady Michelle Obama's leg during a Take Your Child To Work Day event with children of White House staff, in the East Room of the White House, April 22, 2010.

**Opposite Bottom**
President Obama throws a ball for Bo in the Rose Garden of the White House, September 9, 2010.

**Left**
President Obama is joined by the First Lady and Bo, as he delivers remarks during a Christmas holiday reception in the Grand Foyer of the White House, December 15, 2010.

**Right**
President Obama with his daughters, Sasha and Malia, introduce their new dog, Bo, to the White House press corps on the South Lawn of the White House, April 14, 2009.

28000
OBAMA

**Opposite**
Bo Obama, the First Family's dog, waits to board Air Force One on Martha's Vineyard, Massachusetts, en route to Washington, D.C., August 30, 2009.

**Left**
Bo is greeted by several of the President's Active Lifestyle Award achievers in the Diplomatic Reception Room of the White House, November 29, 2010.

**Right**
First Dog Bo lounges in the Palm Room of the White House, September 15, 2011.

**Opposite Top**
At a birthday celebration for Bo, his brother Cappy sneaks a treat from a table in the Rose Garden of the White House, October 9, 2009.

**Opposite Bottom**
Bo sits by a larger-than-life holiday decoration of himself in the East Garden Room of the White House, November 30, 2010. Some 80 volunteers helped create the 4-foot statue, which is made of 40,000 pipe cleaners.

**Left**
Michelle Obama and Bo pose for an official portrait in the White House kitchen garden.

**Right**
Bo pauses for a moment in the Rose Garden of the White House, March 3, 2010.

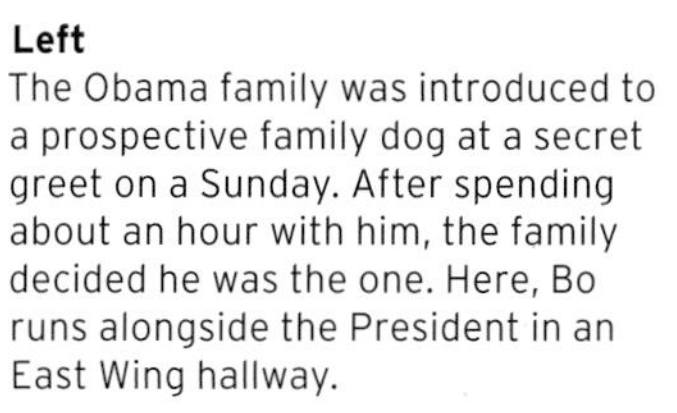

**Left**
The Obama family was introduced to a prospective family dog at a secret greet on a Sunday. After spending about an hour with him, the family decided he was the one. Here, Bo runs alongside the President in an East Wing hallway.

when traveling to Hawaii with their dog, so Bo had to pass a veterinary exam upon landing. And, of course, he did.

When he's at home in the White House, Bo roams the Colonnade, picnics with members of Congress, and patiently waits for the President to finish his meetings. He's helped the First Family welcome guests to official White House events, such as the Easter Egg Roll. White House Grounds Superintendent Dale Haney, who has tended to all First Dogs from the past several administrations, takes Bo on walks. And sometimes Bo surprises tourists as they walk through the White House.

On one occasion, while answering questions from youngsters at an elementary school in Washington, President Obama described going for nighttime walks with the First Dog. He said it's fun, but "sometimes I have to scoop up his poop, because I don't want to just leave it on the lawn!" The response, as one might have expected from a group of kids, was "Eeew!" The President seized the moment to teach a lesson: "If you guys have a dog, you've got to walk your dog, too—and clean up after him."

In the fall of 2011, the White House released an official portrait of Mrs. Obama and Bo in the White House kitchen garden. The director of correspondence, Howli Ledbetter, wrote on the White House blog: "People write in about all kinds of issues. ... But we also get quite a few letters addressed to, or about, the youngest member of the Obama family: Bo! That's why Mrs. Obama recently took a photo with Bo in the White House kitchen garden, so that kids writing in about the garden or about Bo could get a letter back with a photo of the First Dog. Letters from children are always such a joy and inspiration; that's why Mrs. Obama wanted to give them something more tangible in return."

Like the First Dogs before him, Bo has been celebrated at many White House functions, notably in the form of cookies shaped and painted to look like the black-and-white bundle of joy. Christmas is always an affair at the White House, and the First Dog is traditionally included in the décor. Since 1986, a miniature marzipan figure of the First Canine(s) has usually been included in the White House gingerbread house, and Bo is no exception. In 2010, a large replica of the First Dog—made from 40,000 pipe cleaners—welcomed guests as they made their way to the State Floor.

In 2011, even though the theme of the White House Christmas was "Shine, Give, Share", the real star that holiday was Bo. "It's sort of a 'where's Bo?'" First Lady Michelle Obama explained at a White House holiday event with military families. "You've got to find the Bo in every room, because he's hidden everywhere."

The Portuguese water dog was depicted in 1,911 pieces of licorice, in pom-poms, and in 6,850 feet of trash bags. There was a 4-and-a-half-foot-tall Bo made of felt and another replica, just 9-and-a-half inches tall, made of 318 buttons. There were also five topiaries of Bo in the 2011 winter wonderland.

The dog that came to the White House by way of a campaign promise is obviously cherished by the entire Obama family and White House staff, and the nation has fallen in love with him too. As with the First Pets that came before him, Bo plays a valuable role in the everyday lives of his First Family. He provides unwavering companionship and brings happiness and laughter—even during the most stressful of times.

During an interview with Barbara Walters, when asked what person or thing she would want to come back as when she dies, Michelle Obama named her family's Portuguese water dog.

"He's got a pretty great life," she said.

★ PRESIDENT GERALD FORD WITH LIBERTY ★

*"Any man who does not like dogs and want them about does not deserve to be in the White House."*

*President Calvin Coolidge*

# Acknowledgments

For my amazing husband, Bryan, to whom I am eternally grateful for his love and support, thank you.
And to my wonderful parents, Sandy and Mike Boswell, who let me have every pet I ever wanted as a child.

I am also most thankful to the following President, First Ladies, and their families for their participation in this book.

First Lady Barbara Bush
President George H. W. Bush
First Lady Laura Bush
Amy Carter
First Lady Rosalynn Carter
First Lady Hillary Clinton
Tricia Nixon Cox
Patti Davis
First Lady Betty Ford
Susan Ford
Lyndon Nugent
First Lady Nancy Reagan
Lynda Robb

So many talented individuals participated in making this book. Thank you!

Bess Abell
Letitia Baldrige
George Bush Presidential Library - Mary Finch, Bonnie Burlbaw & Rachael Altman
George W. Bush Presidential Library
Jimmy Carter Presidential Library - Polly Nodine
Jennifer Chininis
William J. Clinton Presidential Library - John Keller
Gerald R. Ford Presidential Library & Museum - Nancy E. Mirshah
Whitney Grogan
Hutton Hinson
John F. Kennedy Presidential Library
Lyndon Baines Johnson Presidential Library
Anne MacDonald
Capricia Marshall
Anita & Tim McBride
Roland Mesnier
Nancy Meyers
Melissa Montgomery
Chris Mulder
Eric O'Keefe
Dana Perino
Wren Powell
Ronald Reagan Presidential Library - Michael Pinckney
Ali Rubin
William Seale
Rebecca Sherman
David Sherzer
Brian Smith
Jodie Steck
Charity Wallace
White House Historical Association
Pat & Bubba Wood

# Photography Credits

AP Photo, by Bettmann/ Corbis: Page 21

AP Photo, by Dennis Cook: Page 122

AP Photo, by Eric Draper: Page 170

AP Photo, by Marcy Nighswander: Page 148

AP Photo, by Cliff Owen: Page 200

AP Photo, by William J. Smith: Page 21

AP Photo: Pages 21, 61, 91, 94, 122, 148, 200

Courtesy of the Library of Congress Prints and Photographs Division: Pages 13, 14, 16, 17

Courtesy of the Library of Congress National Photo Company Collection: Pages 13, 16

Courtesy of the Library of Congress Frances Benjamin Johnston Collection: Page 15

George Bush Presidential Library and Museum: Pages 8, 118-143, 147

George W. Bush Presidential Library, photos by Joyce N. Boghosian: Pages 191, 192

George W. Bush Presidential Library, photos by David Bohrer: Pages 185, 188, 189

George W. Bush Presidential Library, photo by Alex Cooney: Page 180

George W. Bush Presidential Library, photos by Shealah Craighead: Pages 183, 184, 186

George W. Bush Presidential Library, photos by Eric Draper: Pages 171-172, 176, 181-183, 195

George W. Bush Presidential Library, photos by Chris Greenberg: Pages 173, 178

George W. Bush Presidential Library, photos by Tina Hager: Pages 6, 173, 177

George W. Bush Presidential Library, photos by Paul Morse: Pages 169, 185, 187

George W. Bush Presidential Library, photos by Jared Ragland: Page 184

George W. Bush Presidential Library, photo by Susan Sterner: Page 174, 180

Jimmy Carter Library: Page 96

Jimmy Carter Library, photo by Jack Kightlinger: Page 93

Jimmy Carter Library, photos by Karl Schumacher: Pages 90, 97

William J. Clinton Presidential Library, photos by Ralph Alswang: Pages 152, 164

William J. Clinton Presidential Library, photos by Barbara Kinney: Pages 144, 145, 150, 151, 154-158, 160, 162, 165

Dwight D. Eisenhower Presidential Library and Museum: Page 20

Gerald R. Ford Library: Page 77

Gerald R. Ford Library, photo by Susan Ford: Page 88

Gerald R. Ford Library, photos by David Hume Kennerly: Pages 71, 73, 74, 76, 80, 81, 84, 86, 89, 222

Gerald R. Ford Library, photo by Jack E. Kightlinger: Page 78

Gerald R. Ford Library, photo by Bill Fitz-Patrick: Page 81

Gerald R. Ford Library, photos by Karl Schumacher: Pages 70, 82, 87

Getty Images, photo by Frances Miller, Time and Life Magazine: Page 44

Getty Images: Pages 210, 212

Lyndon Baines Johnson Library, photo by Mike Geissinger: Page 45

Lyndon Baines Johnson Library, photos by Robert Knudsen: Pages 51, 56

Lyndon Baines Johnson Library, photos by Yoichi Okamoto: Pages 47, 49, 50, 52, 54, 57, 58

Lyndon Baines Johnson Library, photos by Kevin Smith: Page 56

Lyndon Baines Johnson Library, photos by Cecil Stoughton: Pages 48, 51

Lyndon Baines Johnson Library: Page 49

John Fitzgerald Kennedy Library, photos by Robert Knudsen: Pages 22, 23, 25, 26, 30, 33, 36, 40

John Fitzgerald Kennedy Library, photos by Cecil Stoughton: Pages 28, 29, 32, 33, 34, 37, 38, 42, 43

Richard Nixon Presidential Library, photo by Oliver F. Atkins: Pages 63, 69

Richard Nixon Presidential Library, photo by Robert Knudsen: Page 60

Richard Nixon Presidential Library, photos by Karl Schumacher: Pages 64, 67

Ronald Reagan Library, photos by Terry Arthur: Pages 98, 102, 113

Ronald Reagan Library, photos by Michael Evans: Pages 99, 108

Ronald Reagan Library, photos by Mary Anne Fackelman: Pages 101, 105, 111

Ronald Reagan Library, photos by Bill Fitz-Patrick: Pages 104, 109, 112

Ronald Reagan Library, photo by Jack Kightlinger: Page 106

Ronald Reagan Library, photo by Karl Schumacher: Page 116

Ronald Reagan Library, photos by Pete Souza: Pages 108, 110, 114, 115, 117

Franklin D. Roosevelt Presidential Library and Museum: Page 18

Official White House Photo: Pages 216, 217, 218, 220

Official White House Photo, by Samantha Appleton: Page 213

Official White House Photo, by Chuck Kennedy: Pages 196, 203, 208, 214, 218

Official White House Photo, by Pete Souza: Pages 197, 199, 202, 203, 204, 206, 208, 209, 216, 220

Theodore Roosevelt Collection, Harvard College Library: Page 15

White House Historical Association: Page 151

# Bibliography


Bryant, Traphes and Frances S. Leighton. From Truman to Nixon: Dog Days at the White House. New York: Macmillan Publishing Co., 1975.

Bush, Barbara. Barbara Bush: A Memoir. New York: Scribner, 1994.

Bush, Barbara. C. Fred's Story: A Dogs Life. New York: Doubleday & Company, 1984

Bush, Barbara. Millie's Book: as Dictated to Barbara Bush. New York: William Morrow and Company, 1990.

Bush, Barbara. "Millie's Book: The First Dog Dictates Her Memoirs to Barbara Bush." Good Housekeeping Aug. 1990: 95-99. Print.

Bush, Barbara. "Millie's Six-Pack." LIFE May 1989: 32-36. Print.

Bush, George W. Decision Points. New York: Crown Publishers, 2010.

Bush, Laura. Spoken from the Heart. New York: Scribner, 2010.

Carmer, Carl. Pets at the White House. New York: E.P. Dutton & Co., 1959.

Carter, Rosalynn. First Lady From Plains. Boston: Houghton Mifflin Company. 1984. Print.

Cheney, Richard B. and Liz Cheney. In My Time: a Personal and Political Memoir. New York: Threshold Editions, 2011.

Clinton, Hillary Rodham. Dear Socks, Dear Buddy: Kids' Letters to the First Pets. New York: Simon & Schuster, 1998.

Ford, Betty and Chris Chase. The Times of My Life. New York: Harper and Row, Publishers, 1978.

Ford, Gerald R. A Time to Heal: The Autobiography of Gerald R. Ford. New York: Harper and Row, Publishers, 1979.

Kelly, Niall. Presidential Pets. New York: Abbeville Press Publishers, 1992.

"L.B.J.'s Beagles: LIFE Visits Him and Her at the White House." LIFE 19 Jun. 1964: 68A-73. Print.

Reagan, Nancy. My Turn: The Memoirs of Nancy Reagan. New York: Random House, 1989.

Rowan, Roy and Brooke Janis. First Dogs: American Presidents and Their Best Friends. Chapel Hill: Algonquin Books, 2009.

Schank, Katie Marages. White House Pets. Washington, D.C.: White House Historical Association, 2007.

TheWhiteHouse.com

Truman, Margaret. White House Pets. New York: David McKay Company, 1969.

White House Historical Association

Additional information was also compiled from the following presidential libraries:

President George H. W. Bush Library
President Gerald R. Ford Library
President John Fitzgerald Kennedy Library
President Ronald Reagan Library

# Index

This book was produced with recycled, chlorine-free paper made with
10% recovered fiber content, using 100% hydro-electric power.

A portion of the proceeds will be donated to the White House Historical Association.

Printed in Canada.

fifeanddrumpress.com